play like

Au

MW00804161

Stevie Ray Vaughan

The Ultimate Guitar Lesson

by Andy Aledort

To access audio visit:
www.halleonard.com/mylibrary

Enter Code

8721-7843-1553-1435

Cover photo: Clayton Call/Redferns

ISBN 978-1-4803-9050-8

HAL•LEONARD®
CORPORATION
7777 W. BLUEMOUND RD. P.O. BOX 13819 MILWAUKEE, WI 53213

Visit Hal Leonard Online at
www.halleonard.com

CONTENTS

INTRODUCTION

Play Like Stevie Ray Vaughan offers the most in-depth examination of the incredible playing style of the one and only Stevie Ray Vaughan, the immensely influential guitar phenomenon who is rightfully regarded as the greatest blues guitarist of his generation. SRV's complete mastery of the blues and blues-rock idiom is apparent in every single recording he made, from his blistering 1983 debut, *Texas Flood*, to the standout follow-up, *Couldn't Stand the Weather*, through the subsequent releases *Soul to Soul* and *Live Alive* and his brilliant last studio album, the chart-topping, Grammy-winning *In Step*. Since Stevie's untimely passing in 1990, many incendiary discs have been released, such as his duet with brother Jimmie Vaughan, *Family Style*, and the posthumous collections *The Sky Is Crying*, *In The Beginning*, *Live at Carnegie Hall*, the wonderfully intimate *In Session* (with Albert King), *Live at Montreux 1982 & 1985*, and others. With its inclusion of complete transcriptions and essential musical excerpts, this book is designed to clearly illuminate all of the many aspects that made up Stevie's formidable guitar style.

The book is organized into several chapters, each of which focuses on different aspects of SRV's total guitar mastery:

Tale of the Tone

This section delves into the many different pieces of gear that SRV relied upon to create his signature tone, from the modest setup that he used to record *Texas Flood* to the wall of amplifiers and unique array of pedals that became his standard setup soon after and through the rest of his career.

Songs

This section includes complete transcriptions of five essential SRV songs and offers detailed instructional examination of his rhythm and lead guitar work on each. Each of these songs is also demonstrated with an audio track featuring full-band accompaniment.

Essential Licks

Stevie Ray Vaughan developed his signature style through the absorption of every lick that he could listen to by all of the blues and rock guitar greats, from Muddy Waters and Howlin' Wolf to Eric Clapton, Jeff Beck, and Stevie's greatest influence, Jimi Hendrix, as well as the jazz guitarists that he admired, such as Django Reinhardt, Wes Montgomery, Grant Green, and Kenny Burrell. This section breaks down his soloing style by using a collection of the essential licks that he relied upon most often, with audio demonstrations of each lick included in this presentation.

Essential Riffs

One of Stevie's greatest and most enduring strengths as a guitarist was his ability to place his incredible playing style within songs that best showcased his virtuosic abilities. This section details essential riffs from 10 of his greatest recordings.

Integral Techniques

SRV possessed the kind of guitar technique that most players only dream of. In this section, we will break down the intricacies of his brilliant pick- and fret-hand technique.

Stylistic DNA

All of the greatest instrumentalists have a sound that is uniquely their own—distinct and immediately recognizable. In this section, we will look at that aspect of SRV's approach and sound on the guitar.

Must Hear

This section includes the essential recordings for investigation by anyone interested in Stevie Ray Vaughan's incredible legacy.

Must See

There is a great variety of incredible DVDs available showcasing Stevie Ray Vaughan in live performance. This section also details rare videos that can be found on YouTube. Along with dedicated study of the transcriptions and musical examples in this book, watching these performance videos of SRV will provide you with the most complete picture possible of Stevie's utter mastery of the electric guitar.

ABOUT THE AUDIO

To access the audio examples that accompany this book, simply go to **www.halleonard.com/mylibrary** and enter the code found of page 1. This will grant you instant access to every example. The examples that include audio are marked with an audio icon throughout the book.

The equipment used for the audio recording included a custom-made Stratocaster. Originally built in 1987, the guitar features a 22-fret maple neck, designed as a replica of the neck on my 1961 Stratocaster, and an alder body. The pickups in this guitar are Seymour Duncan SSL-1Ls in the neck and middle positions and an SSL-5L in the bridge position. The strings are D'Addario EXL 115s (.011, .014, .018, .028, .038, .049) tuned down one half step. The amplifier is a custom-made Louis Electric KR12 (*http://louiselectricamps.com/guitar-amps/KR_12-amp.shtml*) with a single 12-inch speaker (a Celestion Classic Lead 80) and 40 watts of output, with two EL34 power tubes, three 12AX7 preamp tubes, and one 5AR4 rectifier tube. This is a fantastic-sounding amp and has been a mainstay of my rig for the last year. The amp was miked at the edge of the cone with a Blue en-CORE 100i, and with an M-Audio Solaris positioned six inches in front of the amp. The signals are split hard right (M-Audio) and hard left (Blue).

The only effect pedals used were an original Klon Centaur distortion pedal and a Strymon Lex rotary pedal, designed to replicate the sound of a Leslie speaker cabinet. In regard to Stevie's tone, he used a Fender Vibratone cabinet, which replicated the Leslie sound via a spinning baffle, and the Lex does a great job recreating that specific sound.

TALE OF THE TONE

Hand in hand with Stevie's mind-blowing technique is his gorgeous guitar tone, or more precisely, *tones*. When it came to sculpting a tone that he could call his own, Stevie took a unique approach to every aspect of gear. I can say from extensive first-hand experience that Stevie had the *greatest* live tone that I have ever heard in my life.

First Flight

A great many guitars went through Stevie's hands during his formative years before he settled on a very beat-up 1962/63 "parts" Stratocaster that he would lovingly refer to as "First Wife." The following is a breakdown of the guitars that he started with, progressed to, and ultimately settled upon as his favorites.

Early Guitars

Stevie's first instruments were mostly hand-me-downs from his big brother, Jimmie, a legendary guitarist in his own right, both as a solo artist and as a member of the Fabulous Thunderbirds. Stevie acquired his very first guitar—a very inexpensive gut-string guitar made of Masonite and featuring stencils of cowboys, cows, and rope—as a birthday present in 1961. His first electric was a hand-me-down Gibson Messenger ES-125T, and a little later, he inherited Jimmie's 1951 Fender Broadcaster. In 1969, Stevie got his first Stratocaster—a '63 maple neck. Along the way, other guitars that he used include a few different semi-acoustic Epiphones, a 1954 Gibson Les Paul Junior "TV" model, a 1952 Gibson Les Paul Gold Top, a Gibson Barney Kessel model, and a 1959 Gibson dot-neck 335 (SRV poses with this guitar on the cover of *Soul to Soul*). In the late '70s, Stevie often gigged with a prototype Rickenbacker stereo semi-hollow guitar, which was given to Howlin' Wolf guitarist Hubert Sumlin as a gift in later years.

Primary Guitars

- **Number One (a.k.a. "First Wife"):** SRV acquired this beat-up "parts" sunburst Stratocaster in 1974 from Ray Hennig's Heart of Texas Music, in Austin, Texas. Assembled from parts from different years, the neck is stamped "December '62" and features a "veneer board" rosewood fretboard, and the body is stamped "'63." Also, "1959" is written on one of the pickups, which is the reason why Stevie often referred to the guitar as a '59. Stevie used very heavy string gauges—GHS Nickel Rockers gauged .013, .015, .019, .028, .038, .058—tuned down one half step (low to high: Eb–Ab–Db–Gb–Bb–Eb), akin to Jimi Hendrix, one of his primary influences. Stevie often stated in interviews that he used "the biggest fret wire I could find," such as Gibson bass frets, which, in the early '70s, was not uncommon for guitarists to do. Stevie's guitar tech Rene Martinez has said that all of Stevie's guitars had been re-fretted with "the thickest and highest fret wire I could find with the smallest tang, without using any one specific fret wire." These large frets served to accommodate Stevie's heavy string gauges. Stevie also had all of his guitars modified with five-way (instead of the standard three-way) toggle switches, which afforded him the ability to attain a much greater range of tones from his Stratocasters. Though originally fitted with a standard tremolo system, at some point, it was removed and replaced with a lefty tremolo that remained in the guitar from that point forward. Stevie's manhandling of the tremolo bars resulted in him breaking them frequently, and in later years, he would use custom-made bars that were heavier and could better withstand the nightly abuse.

- **Red:** Stevie bought his stock, red 1962 Strat with the "slab-board" rosewood neck from Charley Wirz at Charley's Guitar Shop in Dallas in 1984. In 1986, Red was refitted with a knock-off Fender lefty neck, and in July 1990, a new Fender neck was installed after this neck was broken in a pre-show accident in New Jersey. When I interviewed Stevie in 1986, he had this guitar strung "upside-down" (i.e., for a lefty) so that he could replicate the way one of his heroes, Albert King, played. "The guitar makes more sense to me when it's strung upside down," Stevie somewhat shockingly told me. "I understand it better and I like playing that way, which is why Red is strung upside-down right now." When asked jokingly if he was considering switching to playing "upside-down" all of the time, he replied, "I just might!"

- **Yellow:** Previously owned by Vince Martell of Vanilla Fudge, this guitar was sold to Charley Wirz, who painted it yellow and gave it to Stevie in the early '80s. The pickup cavity had been completely routed out, so the guitar was virtually hollow inside. Charley fitted it with a single bridge pickup and painted the guitar before giving it to Stevie. This guitar was stolen in 1987 and has never been recovered.

- **Lenny:** His then wife, Lenny, bought this '63/'64 guitar for Stevie in the early '80s. It was stripped down to the natural wood and features a brown stain, as well as a butterfly tortoise-shell inlay in the body. The guitar originally had a neck with a rosewood fretboard but it was soon replaced with a maple neck that was a gift from Jimmie.

- **Butter (or Scotch):** Stevie acquired this '61 slab-board Strat during an in-store appearance in the fall of 1985. The guitar was intended to be a promotional giveaway but Stevie liked it so much that he offered to buy it. The non-original wood-grain pickguard was made specifically for the guitar by Stevie's tech, Rene Martinez.

- **Hamiltone ("Main"):** ZZ Top's Billy Gibbons gave this guitar to SRV as a gift in 1984. Built by James Hamilton, the guitar features a two-piece maple body with a neck-through body design. It originally included EMG pickups, which were replaced with vintage Fender Strat pickups. The fingerboard is ebony with Stevie's name inlaid in abalone.

- **Charley:** This white Strat "parts" guitar with Danelectro "lipstick tube" pickups was made by Charley Wirz and Rene Martinez in 1983 and given to SRV as a gift, with the inscription "More in '84" on the neck plate. It features an alder body and an ebony fingerboard and is a "hardtail" (non-tremolo) guitar with single tone and volume controls.

- **National Steel:** Posing with this guitar for the cover of *In Step*, this 1928 or 1929 National Steel guitar was a gift from roadie Byron Barr, who bought it from Charley's Guitar Shop in 1981.

- **Guild JF6512 12-String Acoustic:** Stevie used this guitar, owned by his friend Timothy Duckworth, sparingly on occasions such as his *MTV Unplugged* appearance on January 30, 1990.

- **Gibson Johnny Smith:** Stevie used this guitar to record "Stang's Swang," and possibly "Chitlins Con Carne" and "Gone Home."

- **Gibson Charlie Christian ES-150:** Stevie used this guitar to record "Boot Hill," released on the posthumous disc *The Sky Is Crying*.

- **Fender Prototype 1980 "Hendrix" Woodstock Strat:** I saw Stevie perform with this guitar at the Mid-Hudson Civic Center in Poughkeepsie, New York, in November of 1986. It had a large upside-down headstock with two string trees but otherwise was set up like a normal Stratocaster. Stevie allegedly bought the guitar in the summer of 1985, prior to performing in St. Paul, Minnesota, at the Riverplace Festival.

Amps

Along his journey from club sideman to international star, SRV's amplifier preferences took him from one to another, ultimately to a majestic wall of amps assembled to deliver the *tone of doom* that is as much a signature of his sound as his virtuosic abilities as a guitarist.

- **1980 Marshall 4140 2x12 Club and Country 100-watt Combo:** Used in the early '80s, either alone or in conjunction with other amplifiers. Refitted with JBL speakers in the early '80s.

- **1964 Fender "Blackface" Vibroverbs:** Stevie often used two Vibroverbs simultaneously; this type of amp remained in his arsenal for his entire career.

- **1964 Fender "Blackface" Super Reverbs:** Stevie typically used two of these amps, along with many others, for live performances. Refitted with EV speakers.

- **Dumble 150-watt Steel String Singer with Matching 4x12 Bottom:** Fitted with 6550 power tubes and four 100-watt EVs. For the recording of *Texas Flood*, Stevie used a single Dumble that was owned by musician Jackson Browne, who also owned the studio where the album was recorded. Shortly thereafter, Stevie acquired a Dumble of his own.

- **Marshall Major 200-watt Head with 4x12 Dumble Bottom:** Fitted with 6550 power tubes and four 100-watt EVs.

- **Late '60s Fender Vibratone:** This amp is essentially the equivalent of a Leslie 16 and features a spinning baffle that creates a vibrato effect. This cabinet can be clearly heard on songs like "Cold Shot" and "The Things (That) I Used to Do." This speaker cabinet was driven by one of the Vibroverbs.

Effects

- **Ibanez Tube Screamer:** Stevie started with the original TS-808, but according to Rene, he used just about every type of Tube Screamer at one point or another, including the TS-9 and TS-10 Classic.

- **Vox Wah:** Stevie preferred original Vox wahs from the '60s.

- **Vintage Dallas-Arbiter Fuzz Face (later modded by Cesar Diaz)**

- **Tycobrahe Octavia**

- **Roger Mayer Octavia**

- **Univibe Univox FM-No 49.5 (used briefly)**

- **Custom-made Splitter Box:** Featured one input and six outputs to send his guitar signal to six different amplifiers simultaneously.

- **MXR Loop Selector:** Stevie used this pedal when playing live in order to take his Tube Screamer in and out of his signal chain.

- **Roland Dimension D:** Used in the studio during the recording of *Texas Flood* and other releases for a subtle chorus-type effect, heard clearly on "Mary Had a Little Lamb," "Texas Flood," "Pride and Joy," and others. As described by engineer/producer Richard Mullen in an interview that I did with him in 2003, "One effect that Stevie liked to use when we mixed *Texas Flood* was this really obscure Roland delay/chorus that gave a little bit of a "growl" sound. It was a stereo device that created phasing effects, which you can hear on the solo to 'Mary Had a Little Lamb' and the end solo on 'Pride and Joy.' During the mixdown, Stevie sat at the board and brought that effect in and out as the song progressed. He used the same effect on *Couldn't Stand the Weather*, too."

- **Fender Medium Picks:** Stevie preferred using the back, or "fat" end, of the pick.

- **Earth III "Music Notes" Straps:** Made by the Music Note Strap Co., started by Richard Oliveri in the late '70s in Staten Island, New York.

SONGS

Tuning Notes

Stevie Ray always tuned down one half step (low to high: E♭–A♭–D♭–G♭–B♭–E♭). Use the accompanying track to tune down to Stevie's pitch so that you will be able to play along with his recordings and the tracks in this book.

Love Struck Baby
From *Texas Flood*, 1983

"Love Struck Baby," the opening track on SRV's debut release, *Texas Flood*, begins as a straight-forward rocker in the style of rock 'n' roll pioneer Chuck Berry. Like the album's closer, "Lenny," this song was written as a tribute to Stevie's wife, Lenny. The rhythm guitar parts on this tune are built from Chuck Berry-style alternating root/5th and root/6th dyads, and Stevie's solos borrow from both Chuck Berry and Berry's greatest influence, the immortal T-Bone Walker. For reference, the song transcription begins on page 11.

Intro

Stevie kicks off the song with two- and three-note chord voicings on the top strings that outline the V ("five") chord, E7, the IV ("four") chord, D7, and the I ("one") chord, A7. For each he adds another voicing that makes reference to the relative diminished seventh form.

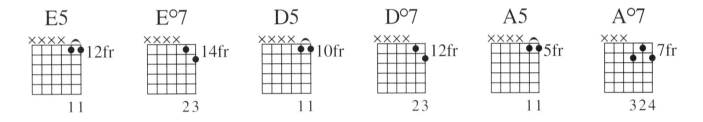

For E7 and D7, he uses a two-note diminished form, whereas for A7, he uses a three-note diminished form. Use all downstrokes with the pick hand when playing this intro (you can try all upstrokes, too, as Stevie would occasionally play the lick this way, or he would switch from all upstrokes to all downstrokes halfway through the lick).

Examples 1–2 offer riffs designed to familiarize you with both the two-note and three-note diminished seventh forms, played in the style and tempo of "Love Struck Baby."

Love Struck Baby Example 1

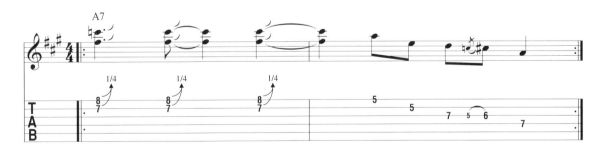

Love Struck Baby Example 2

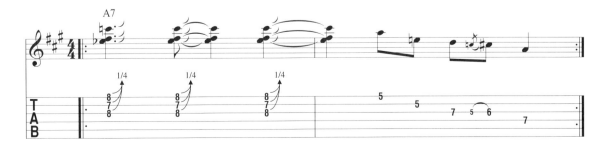

Verse

The verse sections of "Love Struck Baby" rely on standard rock 'n' roll root/5th and root/6th alternating dyads, but Stevie spices things up by adding an unusual dominant seventh voicing for A7 and D7.

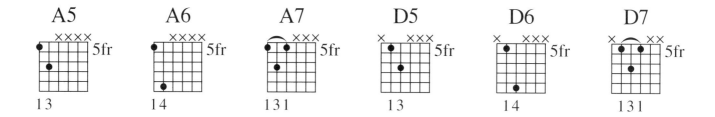

In the transcription, the chord symbols used reflect the overall dominant seventh tonality (A7, D7, and E7). Stevie uses his index and ring fingers to fret the sixth and fifth strings, respectively, when playing the root/5th chords, and reaches up with the pinky to play the root/6th chord. He uses an index-finger barre across the bottom three strings at the fifth fret to play the dominant seventh chords.

Play through Example 3 to get used to switching from root/5th to root/6th over the A7 chord, and then play through Example 4 to work on switching between the two dyads over the D7 chord. Stevie's strumming pattern is very specific as well: he uses a down-down-down-up pattern in steady eighth notes throughout, so strive to use the same picking/strumming technique when playing through these figures and when playing through the transcription.

Love Struck Baby
Example 3

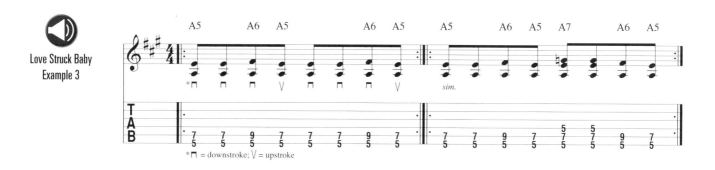

Love Struck Baby
Example 4

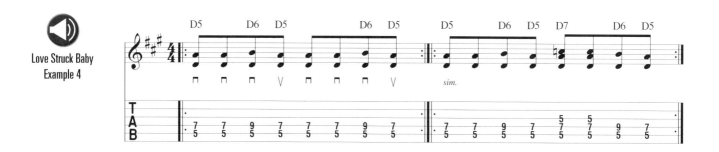

Pre-Chorus

The pre-chorus features all of the same chord voicings that were introduced during the verse section, structured into a repeated eight-bar pattern, illustrated in Example 5. Strive for clear execution and articulation of each note in each chord voicing. The most effective way to master these rhythm parts, and parts like them, is to start slowly and then gradually increase the tempo.

Love Struck Baby
Example 5

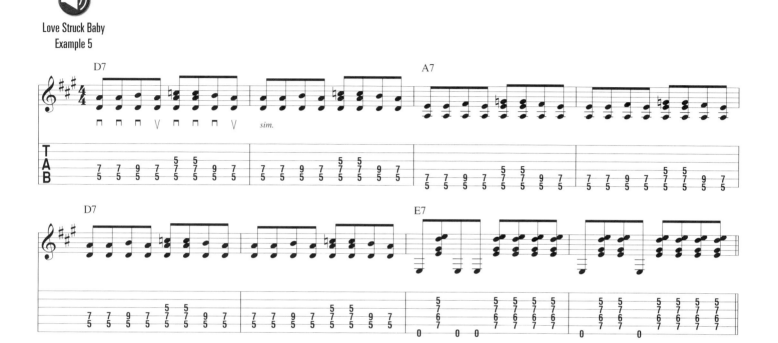

Chorus

The chorus section is derived from the same alternating root/5th and root/6th voicings that are played during the verse and pre-chorus sections, and he inserts the dominant seventh chord into the mix just as often. Once again, use the down-down-down-up strumming pattern that SRV establishes earlier in the song.

Below are the dominant seventh chord voicings that Stevie uses for the "Love Struck" chorus rhythm part.

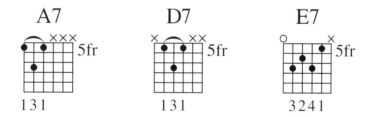

Guitar Solo (First Chorus)

Stevie's entire first solo chorus remains "parked" in fifth position, and in bars 2–3, he relies on the same slightly bent A°7 voicing heard during the song's intro. His lines are primarily based on A minor pentatonic (A–C–D–E–G); notice how he often bends the high minor 3rd, C (first string, eighth fret), up one half step to C♯, the major 3rd. In bar 9, over the V chord, he descends through an A dominant hybrid scale (A–B–C–D–E♭–E–F♯–G) by using two-string barres across the top two strings.

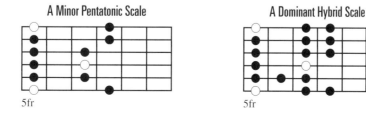

Guitar Solo (Second Chorus)

His second solo begins like the first: with the accentuation of the A°7 chord, but at the end of bar 3, he plays a high A6/9 voicing in 11th position that ascends chromatically to D6/9 in 16th position. At the end of bar 6, he introduces an unusual A9 voicing that is fretted on the top four strings. This voicing is often referred to as the "Hideaway" chord because of Freddie King's prominent use of the chord in that blues classic.

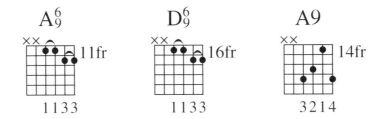

$$A_9^6 \qquad D_9^6 \qquad A9$$

Guitar Solo (Third Chorus)

For the first seven bars of his third solo chorus, Stevie alternates between the A9 voicing and common D9 voicing, spicing things up by swiftly moving chromatically between D9 and C#9.

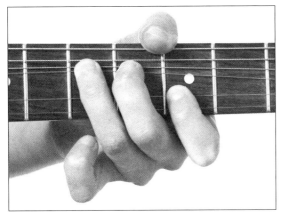

Example 6 illustrates the last four bars of the solo, during which he incorporates the A dominant hybrid scale, as well as *unison bends* on the G and B strings (see photo). While holding E (second string, fifth fret), bend D (third string, seventh fret) up one whole step to E, striking both notes simultaneously to sound a unison bend on the G and B strings.

Love Struck Baby
Example 6

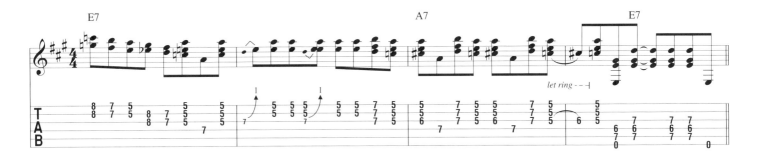

Outro

For the "Love Struck" outro, Stevie reprises the song's intro, moving from E5 to E°7 and D5 to D°7. He wraps up the song in the last two bars by descending through A minor pentatonic, using subtle half- and quarter-step bends on specific notes in the pattern. The song ends on the same high A6/9 chord voicing heard in his second chorus of soloing.

Love Struck Baby
Full Song

LOVE STRUCK BABY

Written by Stevie Ray Vaughan

Tune down 1/2 step:
(low to high) Eb-Ab-Db-Gb-Bb-Eb

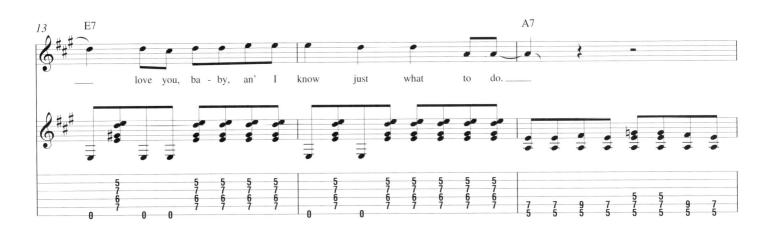

love you, ba - by, an' I know just what to do. ____

Pre-Chorus

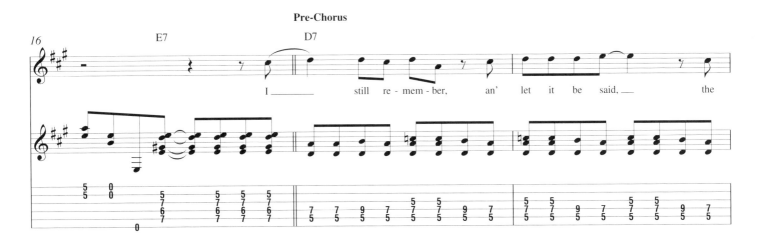

I ____ still re - mem - ber, an' let it be said, ____ the

way you make me feel, it'll take a fool to for - get. I swore a ton of bricks had hit me

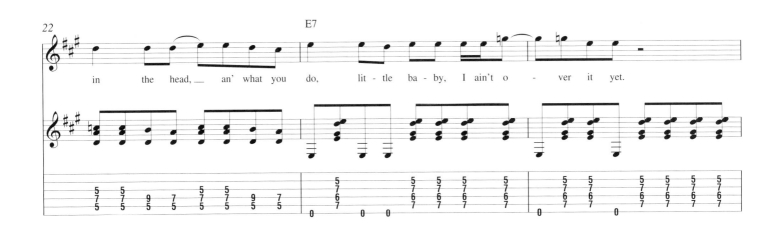

in the head, ____ an' what you do, lit - tle ba - by, I ain't o - ver it yet.

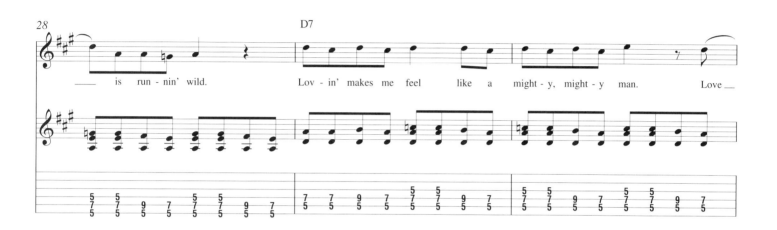

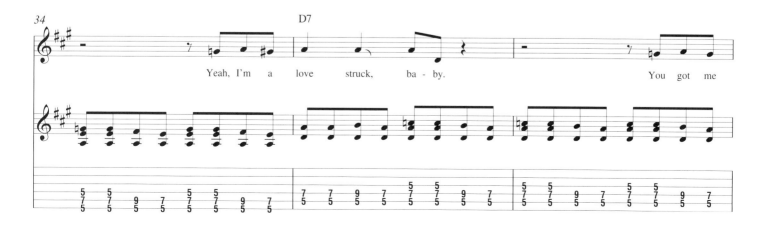

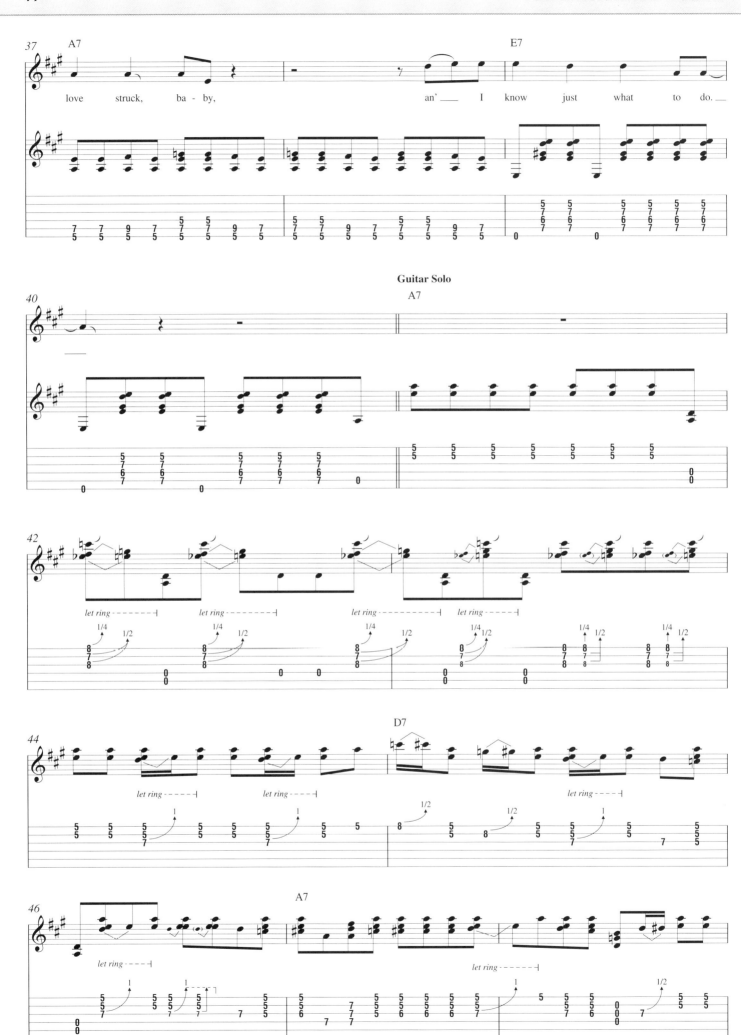

Guitar Solo

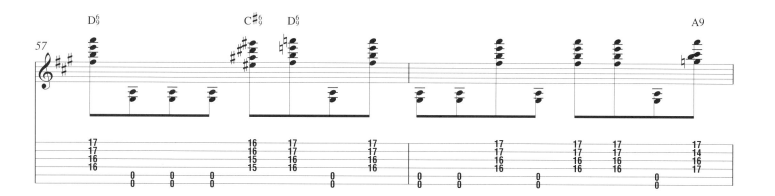

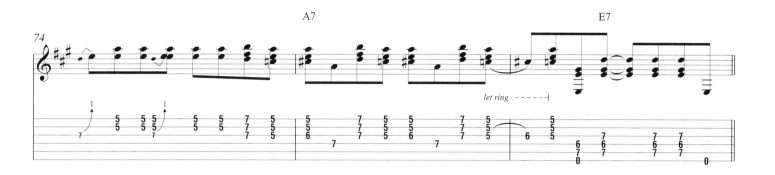

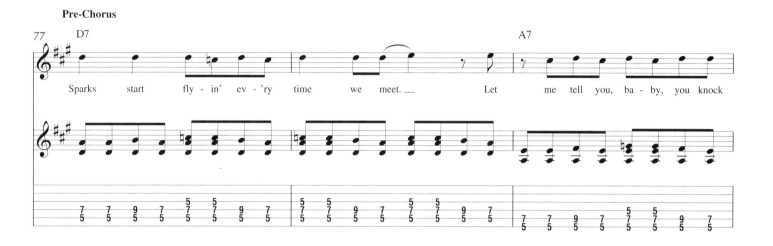

Pre-Chorus

Sparks start fly-in' ev-'ry time we meet. ___ Let me tell you, ba-by, you knock

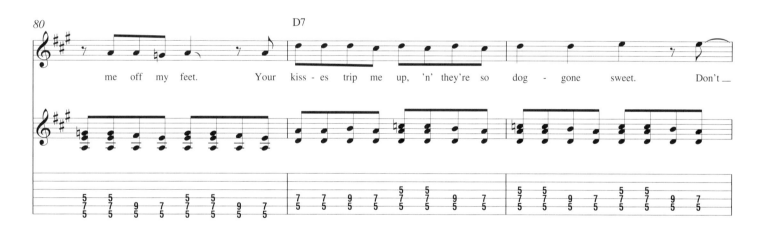

me off my feet. Your kiss-es trip me up, 'n' they're so dog - gone sweet. Don't ___

Chorus

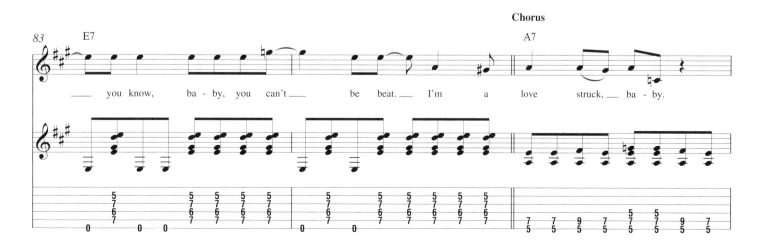

___ you know, ba-by, you can't ___ be beat. ___ I'm a love struck, ___ ba-by.

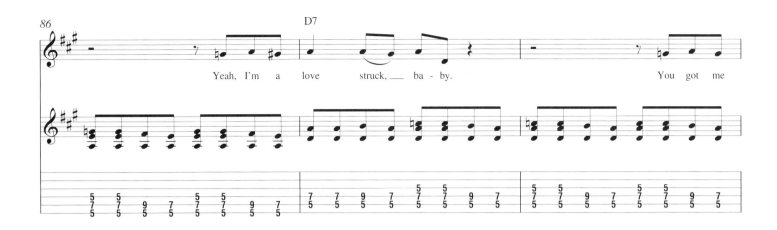

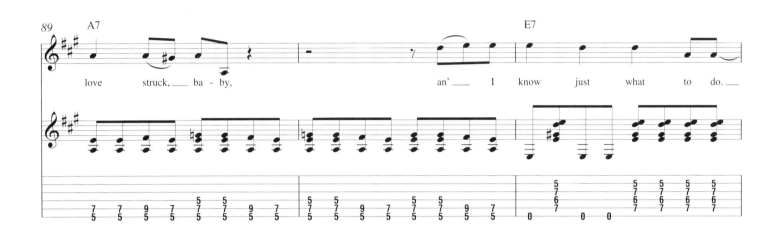

Outro

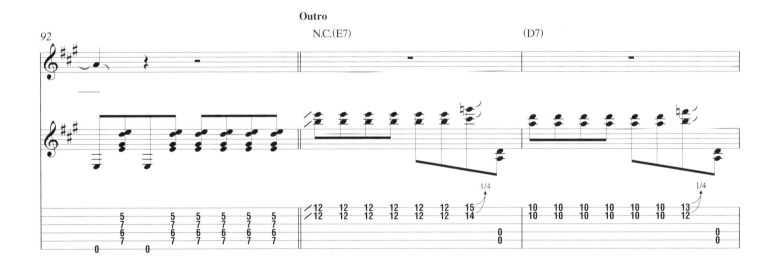

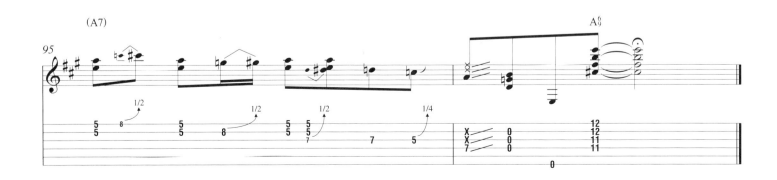

Couldn't Stand the Weather
From *Couldn't Stand the Weather*, 1984

The title track from SRV's second release, "Couldn't Stand the Weather" reveals a strong R&B influence, melding a James Brown-style funk-guitar approach with complex Jimi Hendrix-style rhythm guitar. During the solo sections, Stevie puts his own signature stamp on lines influenced by both Jimi and Albert King. For reference, the song transcription begins on page 22.

Intro

The intro begins in "free time" (no strict tempo). While brother Jimmie Vaughan tremolo-strums the opening chords— Bm, A7, G7, and F#7 (see below)—Stevie adds improvised solo lines (see transcription bars 1–8): over Bm, Stevie sticks with the B blues scale (B–D–E–F–F#–A); over A7, he utilizes the A blues scale (A–C–D–Eb–E–G); and over G7, he utilizes the G blues scale (G–Bb–C–Db–D–F). Strive to recreate Stevie's precise articulation. Over Jimmie's F#7 chord, Stevie plays a first-inversion F#7#9 voicing, which places the 3rd of the chord, A#, in the bass (the lowest note). This unusual chord voicing can also be heard on "Cold Shot."

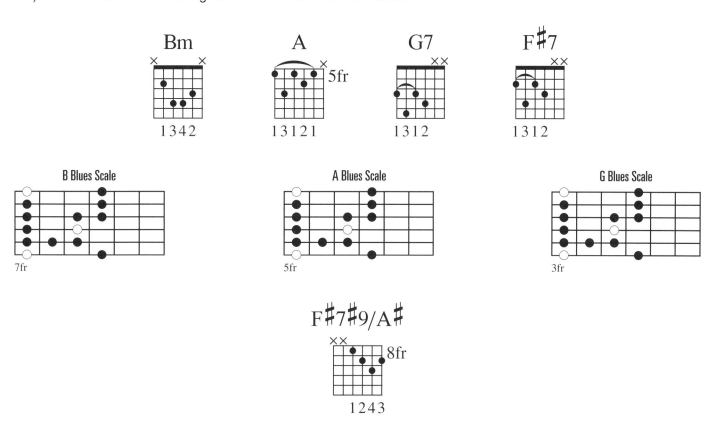

The song then modulates to key of D, the relative major of B minor. A single-note R&B/soul line follows, which the guitar and bass play in unison (see transcription bars 9–19). The line is played four times, although two extra beats are added on the third pass; this is shown as a bar of 6/4 (bar 16 of the transcription).

Couldn't Stand the Weather
　　Example 1

In bars 21–26, Stevie adds a very Hendrix-y rhythm guitar part played in 10th position, and beginning on beat 2, with an F octave fretted on the G and high-E strings strummed in 16th notes. Stevie maintains the rhythmic push of steady 16th notes through most of the pattern by consistently strumming in a down-up-down-up ("one-ee-and-uh") pattern.

At the end of bar 21, barre your middle finger across the G and B strings at the 12th fret and then bend and release them one half step; as the notes are held into the next barre, add subtle vibrato. A useful tip is to keep your fret-hand thumb wrapped over the top of the fretboard throughout, fretting the low-D root note at the 10th fret of the sixth string. Stevie incorporates this low root note into the lick in a few essential spots, akin to Jimi Hendrix on his songs "Freedom" and "Izabella." Stevie plays variations on the idea each time through, so try playing Example 2 repeatedly in order to get a handle on the different fretting and strumming techniques used to execute the riff.

Couldn't Stand the Weather
Example 2

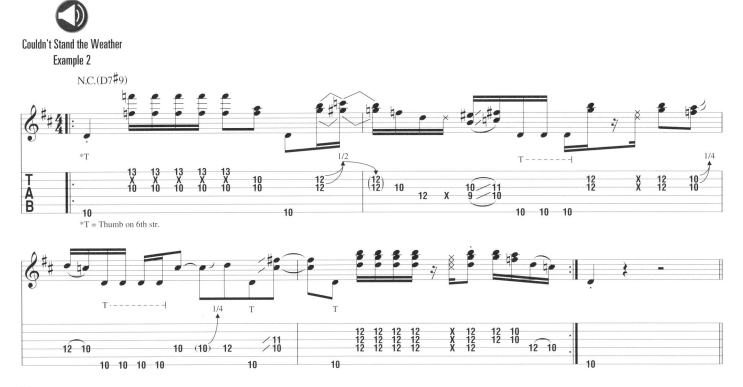

Verse

Through the first eight bars of the verse, Stevie strums a 16th-note-based syncopated rhythm on a static Dm7 chord (see below). The best way to execute this rhythm part is to strum across all of the strings in steady 16th notes by using a consistent down-up alternating pattern. Release fret-hand pressure on the strings wherever X's are indicated in the written music in order to intersperse the muted-string accents.

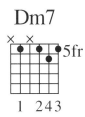

In bars 9–16, he switches to arpeggiations of the intro chords: Bm, A7, G7, and F#7#9 (see below). An *arpeggio* is sounded when the notes of a chord are played individually and in succession.

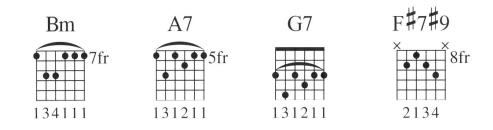

Over Bm, he adds brief lines based on B minor pentatonic (B–D–E–F♯–A). The song then moves to the interlude, which is a restatement of the funky rhythm part that closed out the intro, as shown in Example 2. This is then followed by the second verse and a restatement of the rhythm part played during the first verse.

Guitar Solo

Bars 1–15 of the guitar solo are based on D minor pentatonic (D–F–G–A–C). Notice that Stevie relies on many phrases played in eighth-note triplets, wherein three notes fall evenly within a given beat. In bars 16–27, he switches to lines based on B minor pentatonic (B–D–E–F♯–A) and picks the notes fretted on the high E string with a pick-hand finger, snapping the string against the fretboard à la Albert King.

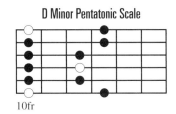

D Minor Pentatonic Scale

10fr

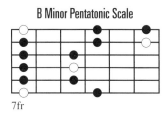

B Minor Pentatonic Scale

7fr

Example 3 offers an example of how to incorporate fingerpicking into a single-note riff in the style of Albert King.

Couldn't Stand the Weather
Example 3

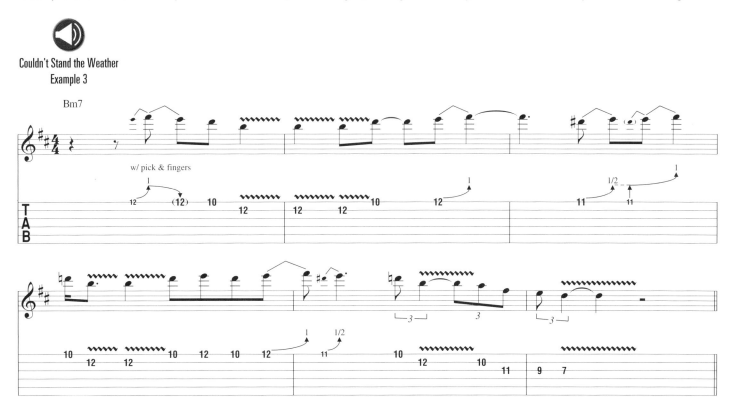

In bars 28–29, Stevie moves to lines based on G minor pentatonic (G–B♭–C–D–F), and the section culminates with syncopated strumming on the F♯7♯9 chord.

Outro

Here, SRV revisits the funky Hendrix-inspired rhythm part alluded to in Example 2. Notice the slight variations that he adds each time he runs through the four-bar figure. The song ends with a fast trill between C (fifth string, third fret) and D (fifth string, fifth fret), followed by bass-string riffs based on D minor pentatonic (D–F–G–A–C).

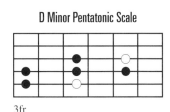

D Minor Pentatonic Scale

3fr

COULDN'T STAND THE WEATHER

Words and Music by Stevie Ray Vaughan

Couldn't Stand the Weather
Full Song

Tune down 1/2 step:
(low to high) Eb-Ab-Db-Gb-Bb-Eb

Intro
Free time
Bm

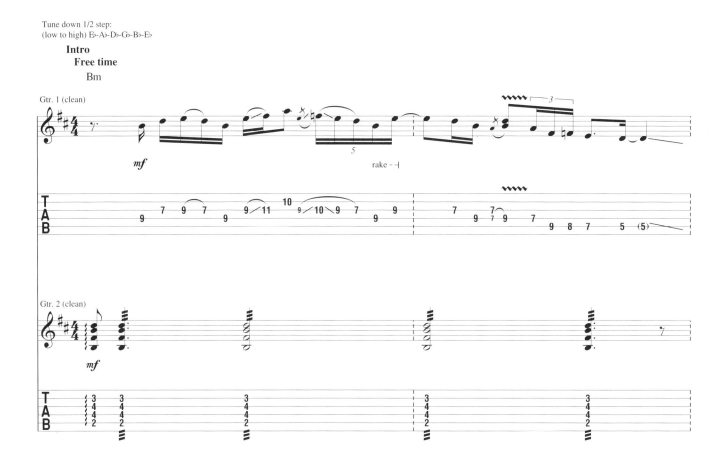

A7

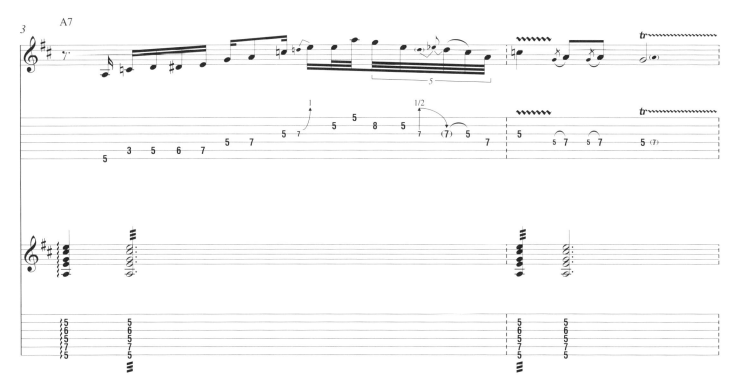

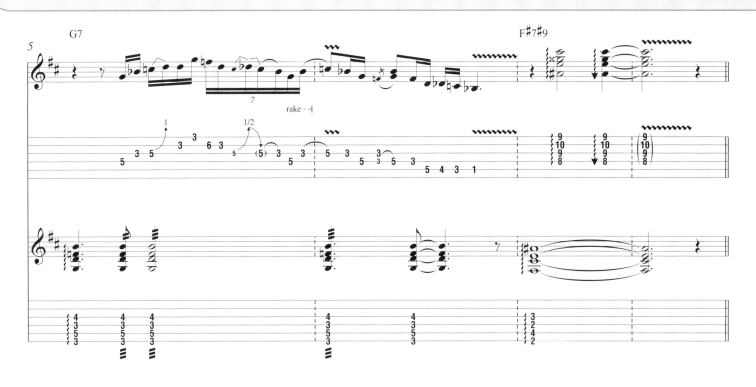

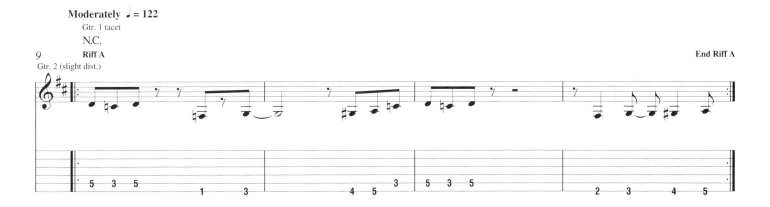

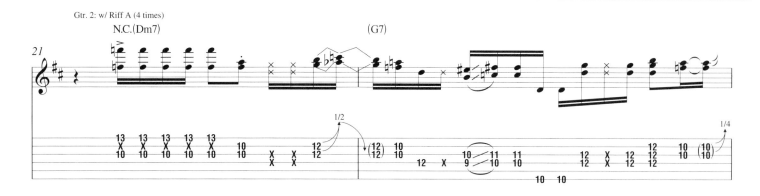

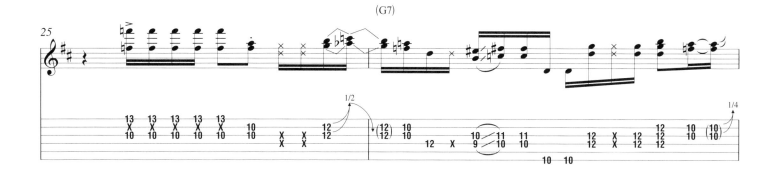

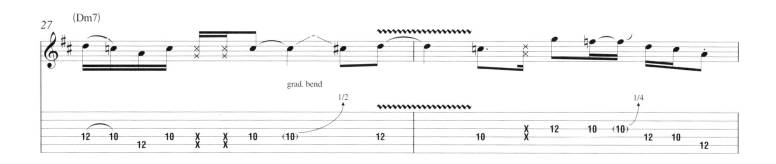

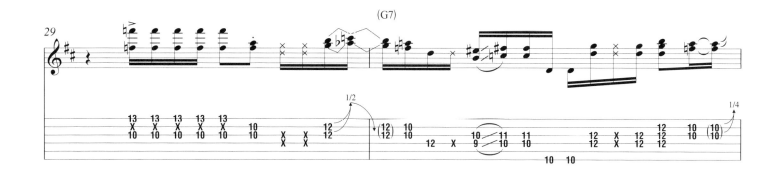

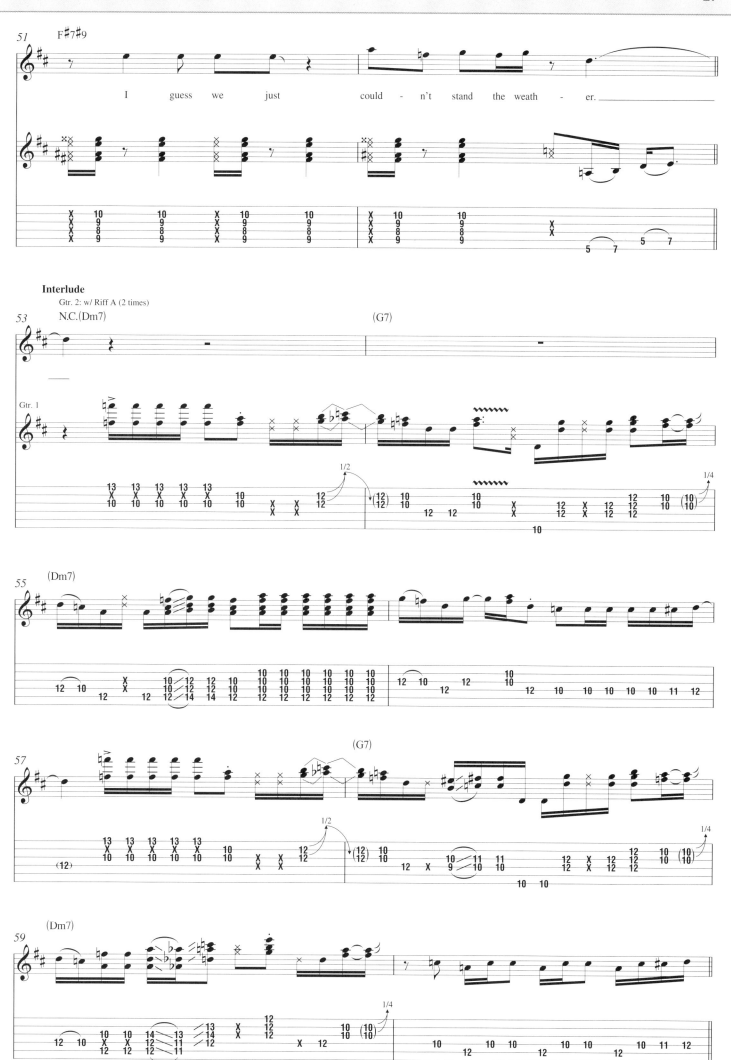

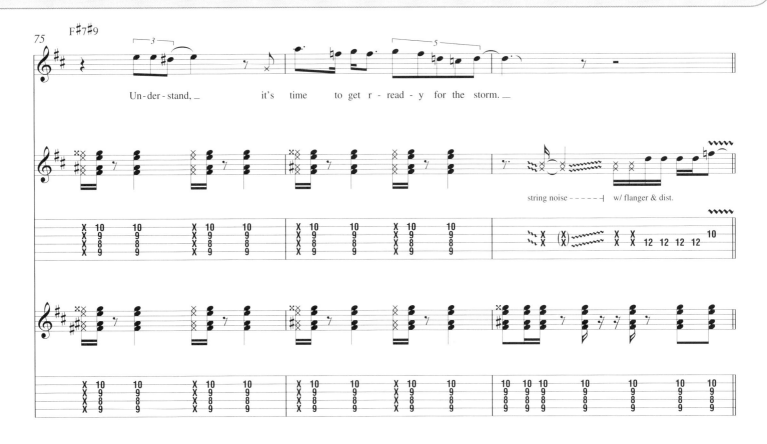

Un-der-stand, ___ it's time to get r-read-y for the storm. ___

string noise - - - - - -⊣ w/ flanger & dist.

Guitar Solo
Gtr. 2: w/ Rhy. Fig. 1 (7 1/2 times)

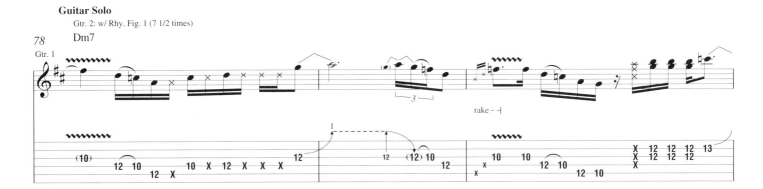

rake -⊣

steady gliss.

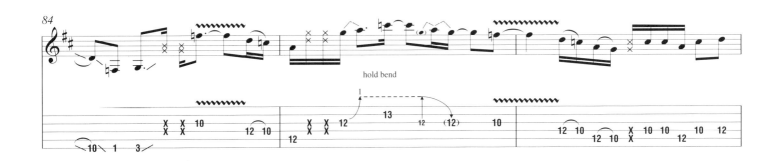

hold bend

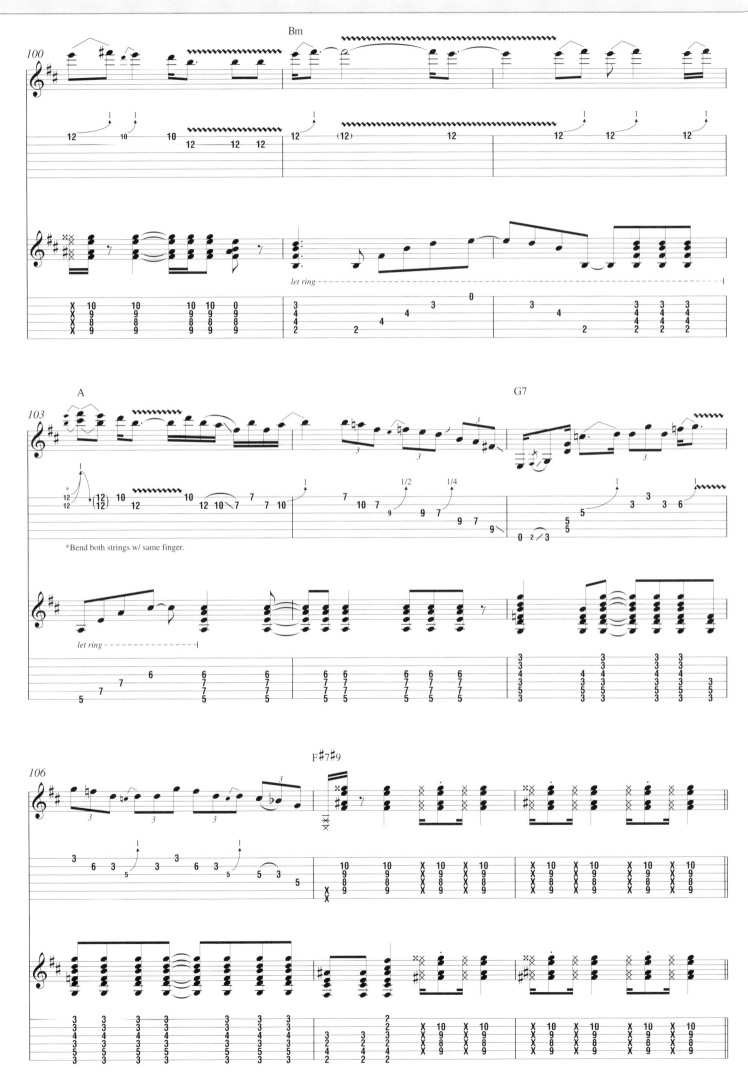

*Bend both strings w/ same finger.

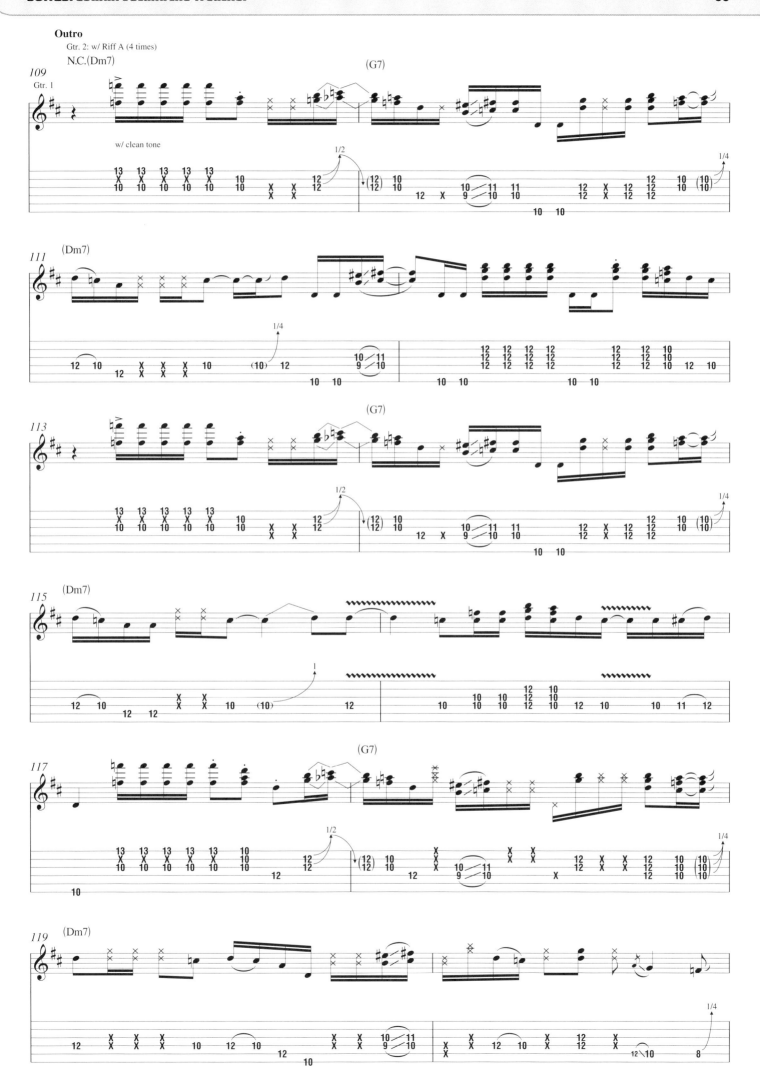

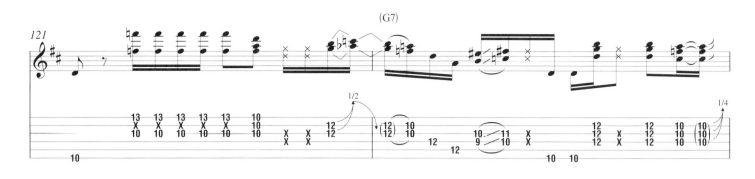

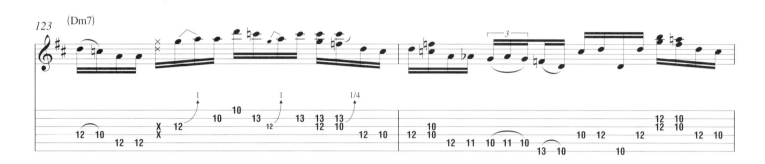

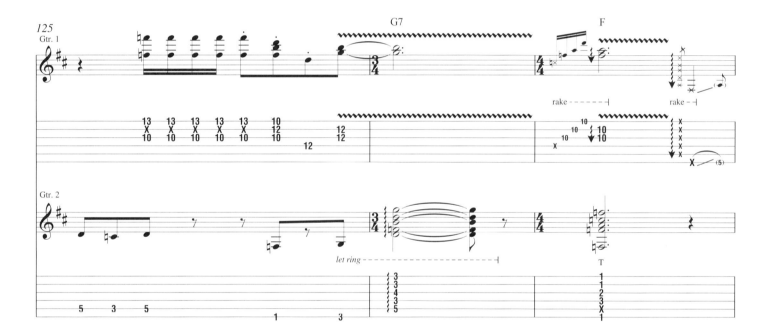

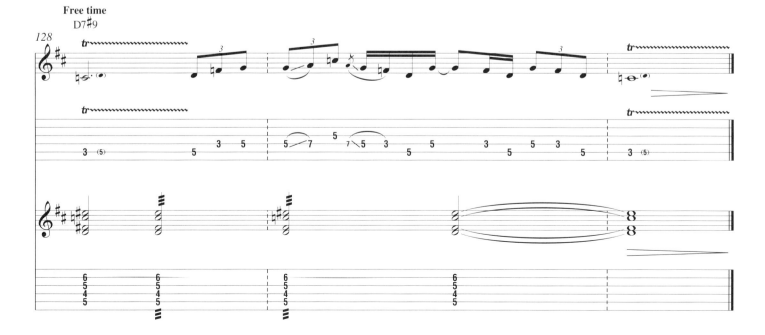

Texas Flood
From *Texas Flood*, 1983

Along with Jimi Hendrix, Stevie's greatest influence was Albert King, a blues guitar giant who played left-handed with the guitar strung upside down (in reverse order, with the lowest-pitched string closest to the floor) while also tuning down one-and-a-half steps. Detuning in this way allowed Albert to utilize extremely wide string bends that are very difficult to recreate on a normally strung—and normally tuned—guitar. Stevie came closer than anyone to recreating Albert's licks authentically, which was acknowledged by Albert in the great friendship that they developed. For reference, the song transcription begins on page 38.

Intro

Apparent throughout this excellent track is Stevie's ability to fuse absolute technical precision with deep emotional feeling, delivering a performance of pure power and brilliance. The majority of the track is brimming with Albert King-style phrasing, tone, and attack, accentuated by pick-hand fingerpicking wherein the strings are "snapped" against the fretboard, yielding a sharp and aggressive sound. Also in evidence is the influence of T-Bone Walker, especially via the inclusion of the 9th (A in the key of G) and the ♭9th (A♭ in the key of G) within the scale structure of the G blues scale (G–B♭–C–D♭–D–F).

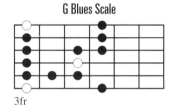
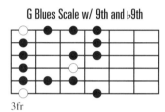

During the first two bars of the song, Stevie relies on "B.B. King-approved" sixth chords, as well as ninth chords, to outline the I (G) and IV (C) chords.

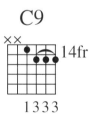

Stevie "crams" fast flurries of notes into the slow-blues groove, making for some very complex phrases that can be a bit difficult to read. Listen closely to the recording and dissect each bar one beat at a time, scrutinizing the internal phrasing within each eighth-note triplet.

Example 1 on the next page illustrates bars 3–5 of the intro; notice the smooth delivery that is locked into the beat, as well as the deft use of bends, hammer-ons, pull-offs, and slides. Also of note is the use of the signature slow, wide vibrato, executed by shaking the entire guitar while holding the fret-hand steady. Mastering these phrases will have you well on your way to grasping SRV's approach to soloing over a slow blues.

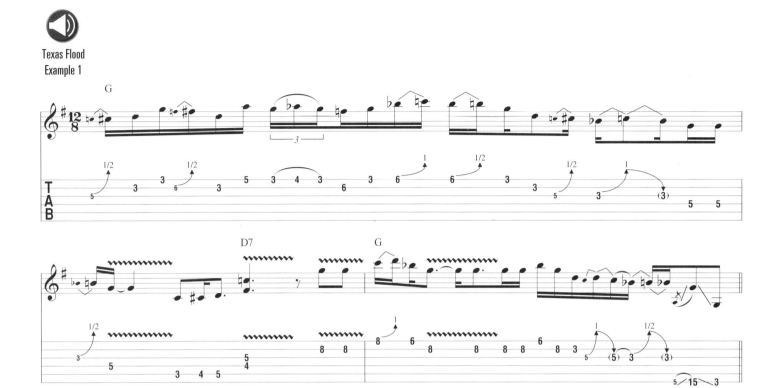

Texas Flood
Example 1

Verses

During the "Texas Flood" verse sections, SRV uses the standard slow-blues approach of backing his vocal lines with spare chords and then playing long, improvised, single-note lines between the vocal phrases in what is known as "call and response." The chords used are G6, C9/G, and D7. Again, the solo lines are based on the G blues scale with the inclusion of the 9th and ♭9th.

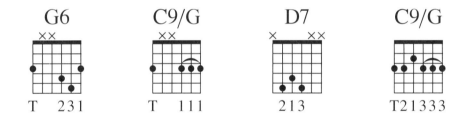

Guitar Solo (First Chorus)

Stevie relies on many of the same phrasing concepts used during the intro and verse sections for his improvised lines during his two choruses of soloing. He accentuates the notes of G minor pentatonic in sixth position, and in bar 7 of the first chorus, briefly shoots up to G minor pentatonic in 15th position (with the inclusion of B natural, the major 3rd). Once again, read through these phrases slowly and carefully in order to recreate the lines with rhythmic precision, as well as with clear, distinct articulation.

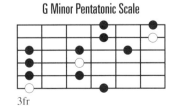

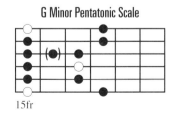

Guitar Solo (Second Chorus)

The unearthly multi-string bends that Stevie executes at the start of the second chorus are staples of the Albert King sound, wherein two or three strings are fretted simultaneously with just a single fret-hand finger (see photo). Executing these multi-string bends properly requires great fret-hand strength, as well as diligent practice.

Before trying to replicate the lines that Stevie plays in his solo, practice playing through Example 2, wherein two strings are fretted and bent with a single fretting finger.

Texas Flood
Example 2

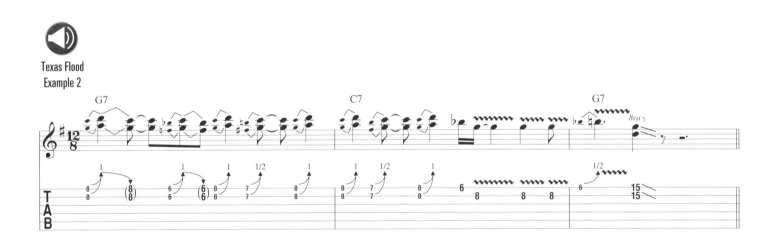

Outro (Last Verse)

Stevie utilizes the same basic approach here as the other verses, playing improvised phrases between the chords and vocal lines that are, in many cases, virtually identical to the lines that he played during verses 1 and 2. Once again, listen closely to the signature elements of his playing style; in particular, his *phrasing* and *touch*. Like all of the true blues guitar greats, Stevie Ray Vaughan was able to communicate deep feeling in his guitar playing, and nothing illustrates this better than his performances within the slow-blues format.

TEXAS FLOOD

Words and Music by Larry Davis and Joseph W. Scott

Texas Flood
Full Song

Tune down 1/2 step:
(low to high) E♭-A♭-D♭-G♭-B♭-E♭

Intro
Slow Blues ♩ = 60

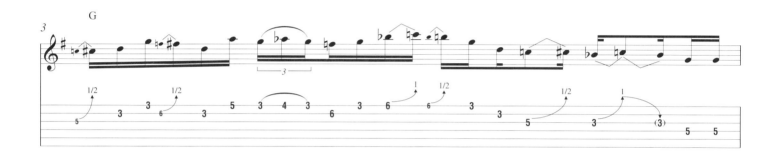

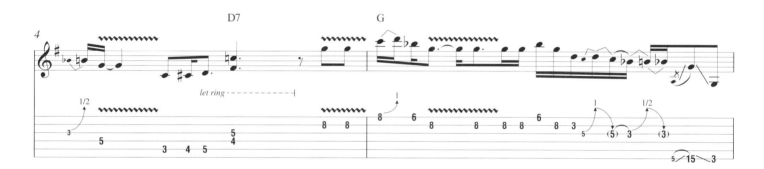

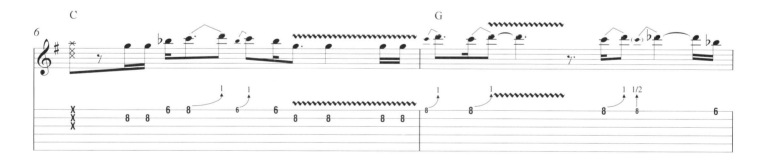

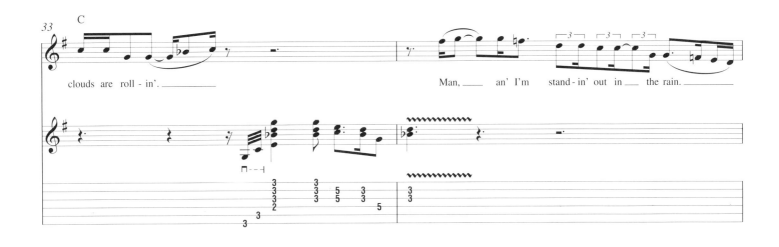

clouds are roll-in'.   Man,____ an' I'm stand-in' out in___ the rain.____

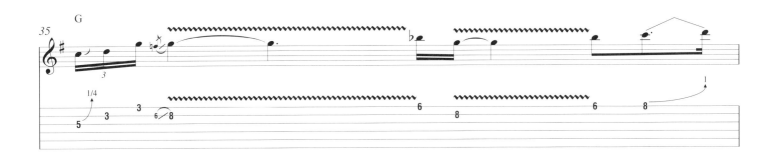

Yeah,_____ flood_____

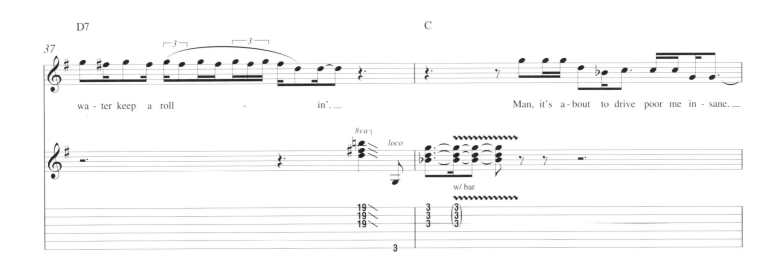

wa-ter keep a roll   -   in'.___   Man, it's a-bout to drive poor me in-sane.___

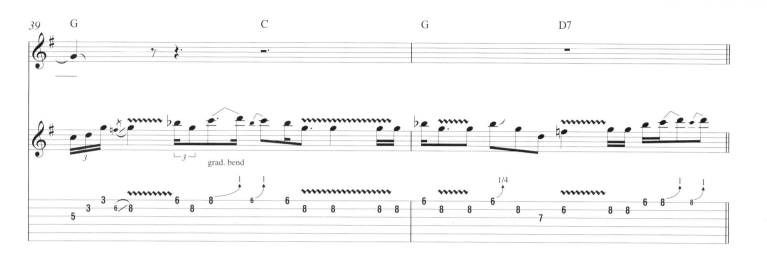

Guitar Solo

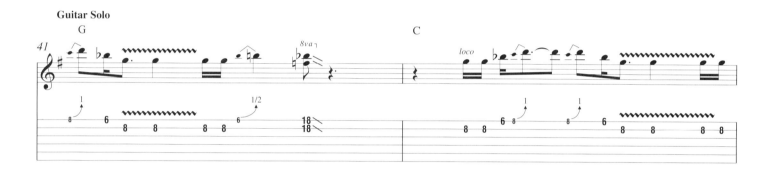

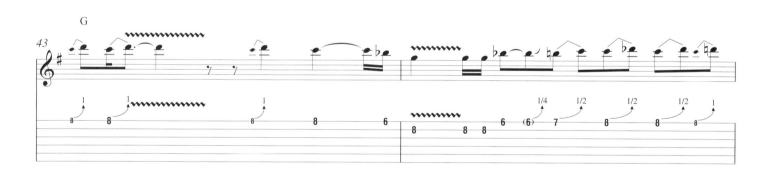

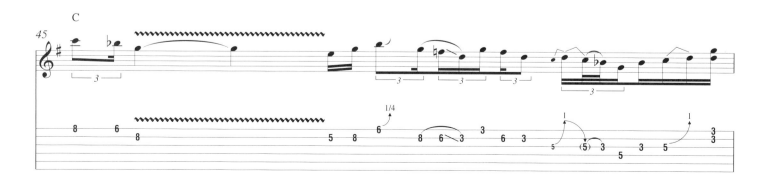

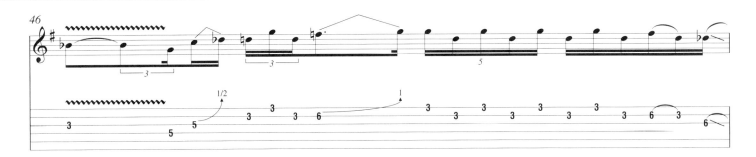

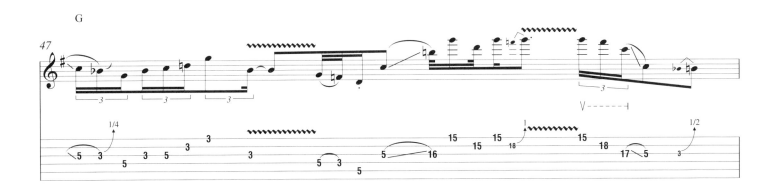

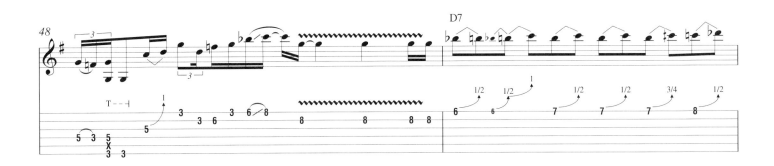

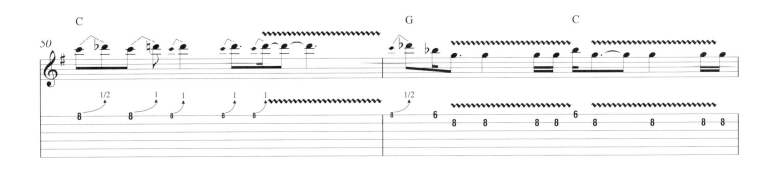

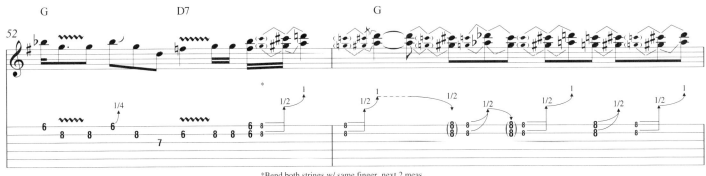

*Bend both strings w/ same finger, next 2 meas.

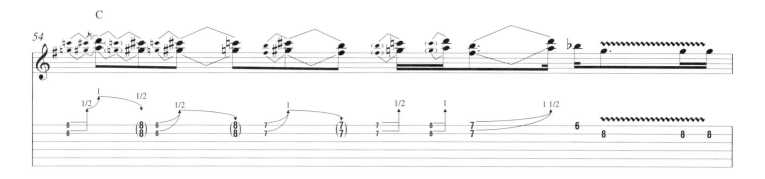

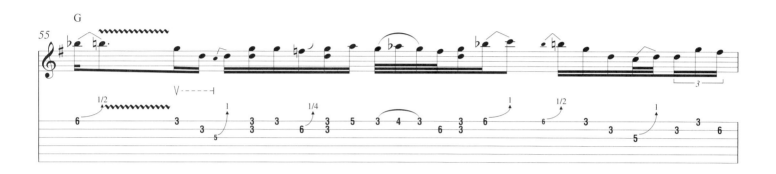

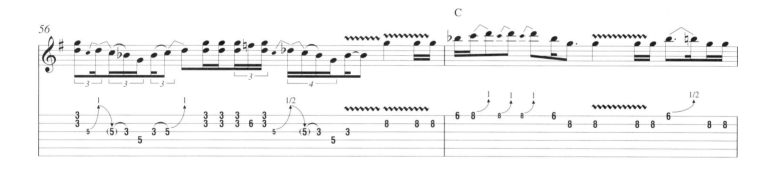

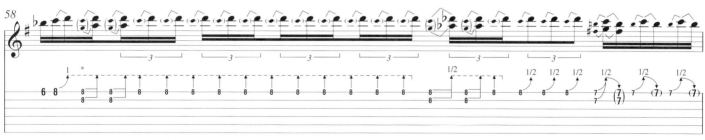

*As before, this measure only.

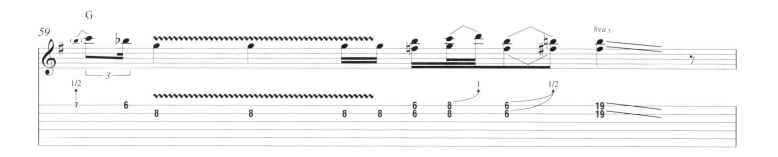

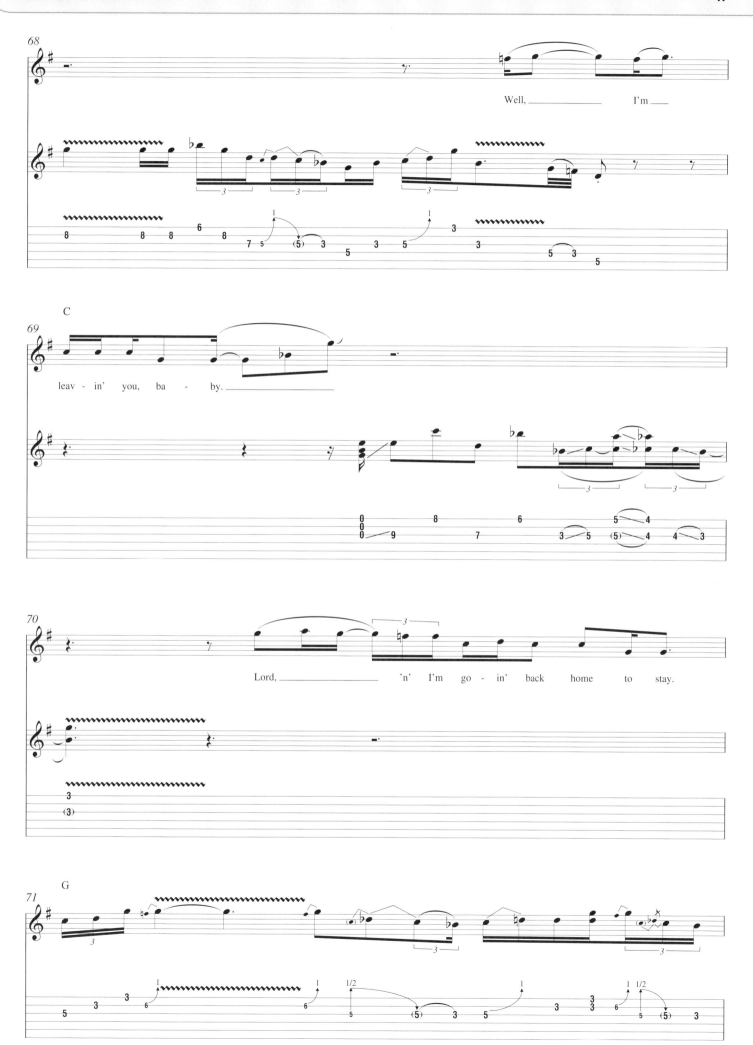

Pride and Joy
From *Texas Flood*, 1983

"Pride and Joy" is a hard-driving blues shuffle in E that would become the primary hit song from Stevie's debut release, *Texas Flood*. His aggressive pick-hand attack, combined with his crystal-clear tone and super-heavy string gauges, provide his guitar parts with an incredible *presence* unlike any other rock or blues player. This track also showcases Stevie's rock-solid connection to *time* and *groove*—he was one of the few guitarists that drove the beat of the song harder than even the drummer, and "Pride and Joy" offers great evidence of this fact. For reference, the song transcription begins on page 53.

Intro

The song opens with a powerful signature lick based on E minor pentatonic (E–G–A–B–D), played in a "Texas" style not unlike Texas blues great Lightnin' Hopkins. When he adds additional single-note licks at the end of the intro, he leans on the E blues scale (E–G–A–B♭–B–D).

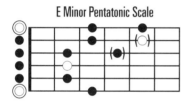

E Minor Pentatonic Scale

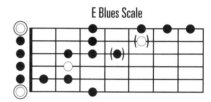

E Blues Scale

The very first bar of the intro is slightly deceptive in that the lick comes in on the upbeat of beat 1, so the very first sound you hear should be thought of as "and," followed by "2-and, 3-and, 4-and." The subsequent two-note lick that is played on the top two strings at the seventh fret falls squarely on the downbeat of beat 1 (bar 2).

At the start of the first 12-bar form (bar 5), Stevie introduces the songs primary "theme": a single-note bass-line riff played on the wound strings, with upbeat accents on the top three strings, played open.

Example 1 illustrates the bass-line riff that falls on strings 6–4 in isolation so that you will be able to clearly focus on learning this pattern.

Pride and Joy
Example 1

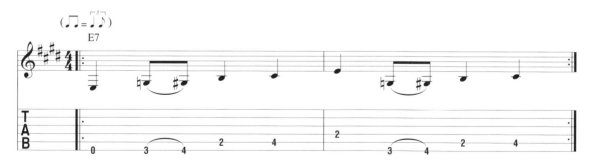

Example 2 illustrates just the upbeat accents on the top three strings, while Example 3 combines the two elements, forming the "Pride and Joy" signature riff. The only tricky part of the lick is employing the hammer-on from G to G# on beat 2: when the G# is sounded, the top three strings must be sounded simultaneously. When playing over the IV chord, A7, the lick is simply shifted to strings 5–3.

Pride and Joy
Example 2

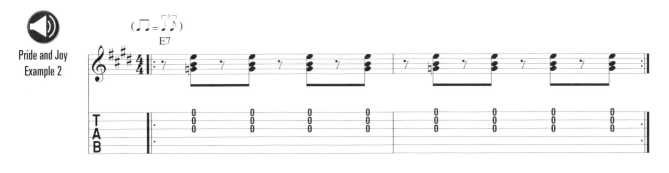

Pride and Joy
Example 3

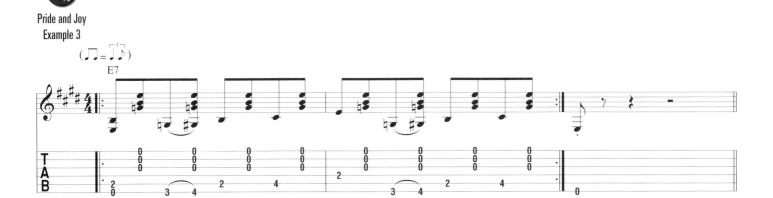

Verse

Through the first four bars of most of the verse sections of the song, SRV sounds only the top-string upbeat accents, adding concise licks based on the E blues scale at the end of bar 2. On the IV chord, A7, he plays a standard second-position "cowboy" chord voicing (see below). In bars 9–10, over the V chord, B7, and IV chord, A7, respectively, he transposes the signature riff to the root note of each chord. In bar 11 of the first verse, he employs an upstroke "rake" across the top three strings, dragging the pick from high to low. Be sure to allow all of the notes to ring clearly when executing this signature element of the single-note phrasing.

A7

During the second verse, he alternates A6/E and E chords in bars 7–8.

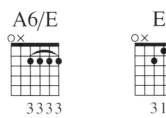

A6/E   E

"Break Verses"

Also commonly referred to as a "stop chorus," the third and fourth verses of "Pride and Joy" feature an abrupt stop on beat 1 of bars 1–3. As shown in Example 4, E major chords are alternated against a riff based on E minor pentatonic, played on the top four strings and featuring a fast bend/release/pull-off on the G string. The proper execution of this lick requires strength and precision in bending and releasing, so practice this phrase slowly and then gradually increase the tempo.

Pride and Joy
Example 4

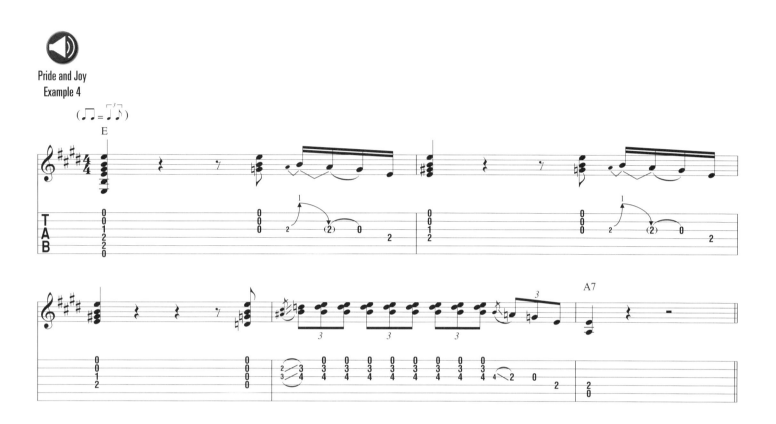

Guitar Solo

In the first and second choruses of his guitar solo, Stevie utilizes the standard Delta blues technique of allowing open strings to ring while playing single-note riffs and/or double stops (two-note shapes), resulting in a wider, fatter sound. In the key of E, it is common to utilize the open high-E string in this manner, which Stevie does while playing various two-note figures on the G and B strings. When played as eighth-note triplets (such as in bars 1–3 of his first solo chorus), SRV often uses upstrokes exclusively in order to accentuate the sound of the open high-E string.

During the first solo chorus, SRV plays through bars 4–7 with the E minor pentatonic scale in 12th position (see below). For the majority of the soloing throughout these first two solo choruses, he relies on the open-position E minor pentatonic and E blues scales that were introduced in the intro section.

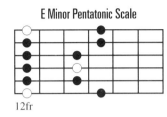

The second solo chorus reprises the phrases introduced during the intro, starting with the unison high-E notes, combining the open high-E string with E note at the fifth fret of the second string. In bars 1–4, he alternates between the unison Es and a simple two-note figure (also on the top two strings) that includes a slight quarter-step bend.

Over A7, Stevie slides into E and G on the third and second strings, respectively, again including the open high-E string. This riff makes direct reference to A7, as G is the minor (dominant) 7th of the chord.

Outro Guitar Solo

Stevie's outro solo begins with sliding two-note shapes fretted on the second and third strings that are sounded along with the open high-E string. Strumming in eighth-note triplets, he moves through several positions: third, fifth, 12th, and 15th.

The remainder of the lines are primarily based on E minor pentatonic (E–G–A–B–D), and he ends the songs with an aggressive E7♯9 chord and wide, whammy bar-induced vibrato.

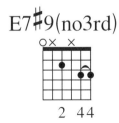

PRIDE AND JOY

Written by Stevie Ray Vaughan

Pride and Joy
Full Song

Tune down 1/2 step:
(low to high) Eb-Ab-Db-Gb-Bb-Eb

Intro
Moderately ♩ = 122

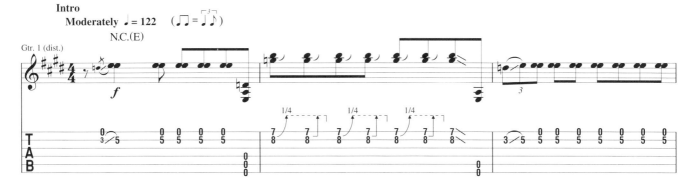

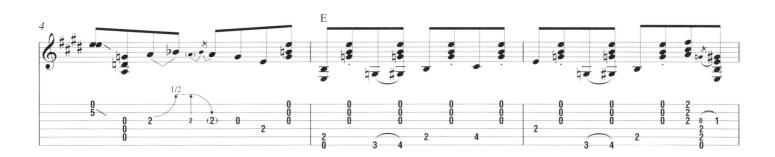

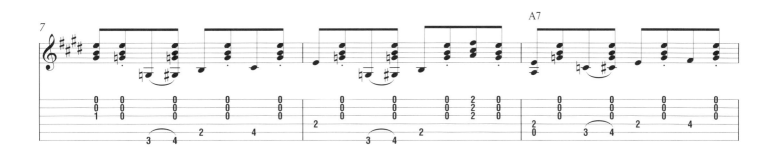

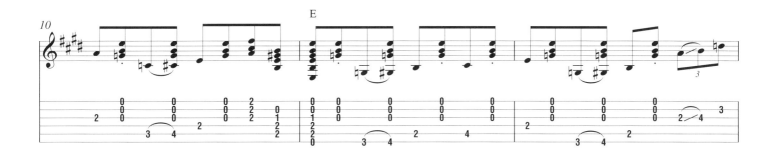

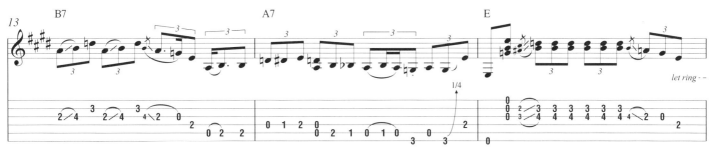

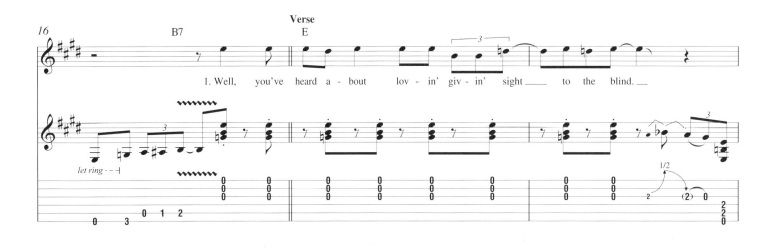

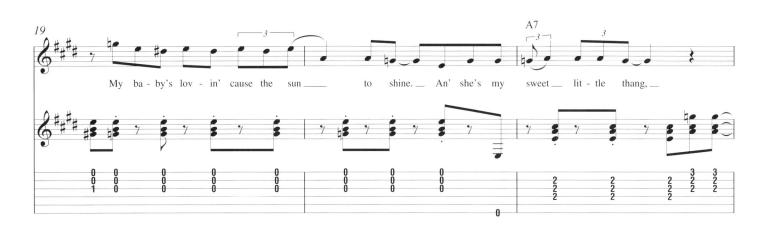

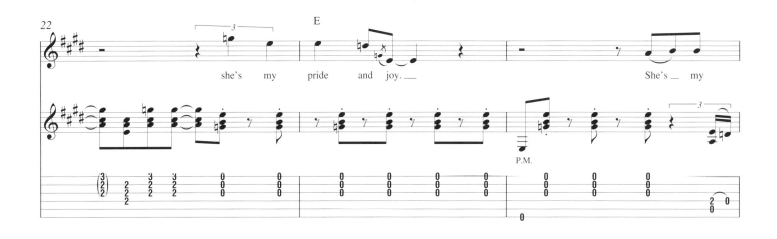

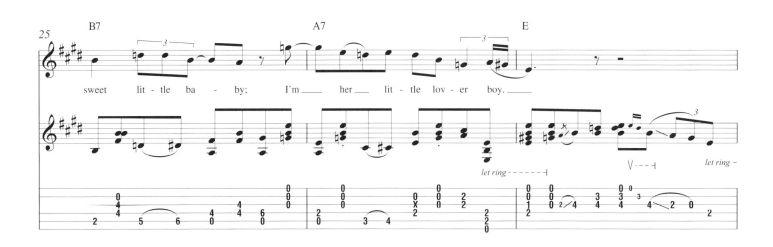

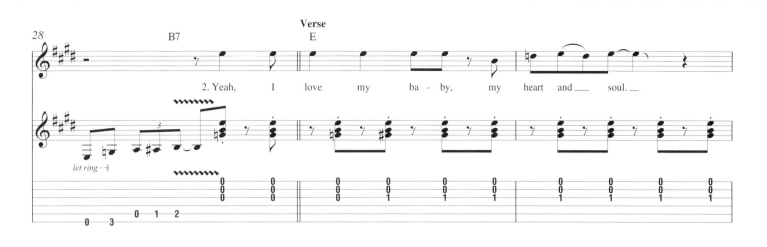

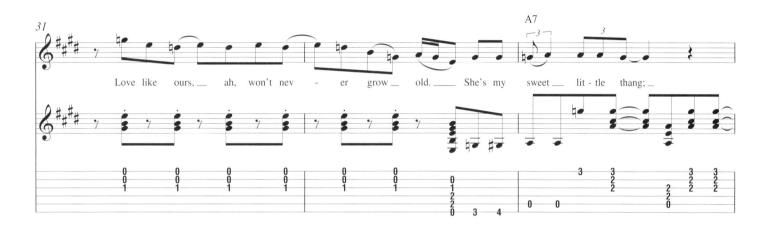

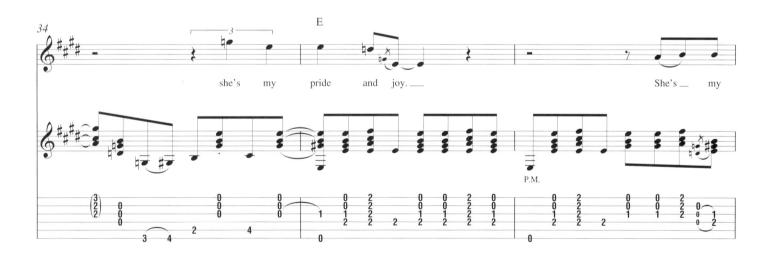

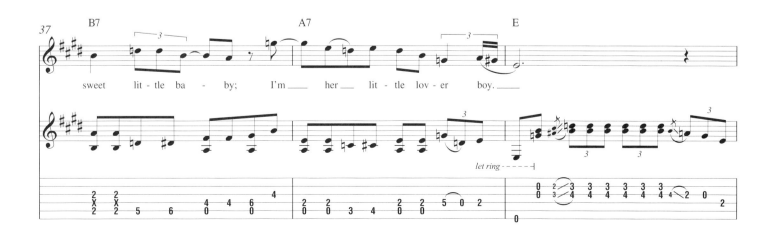

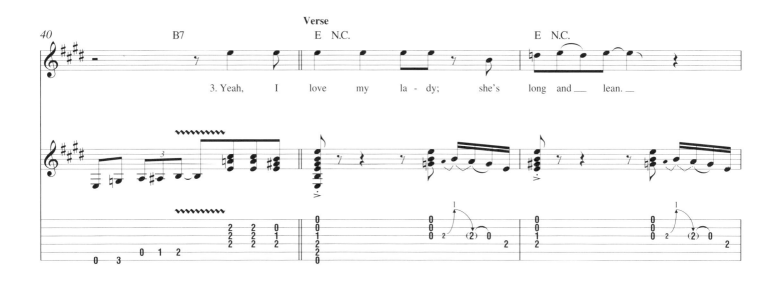

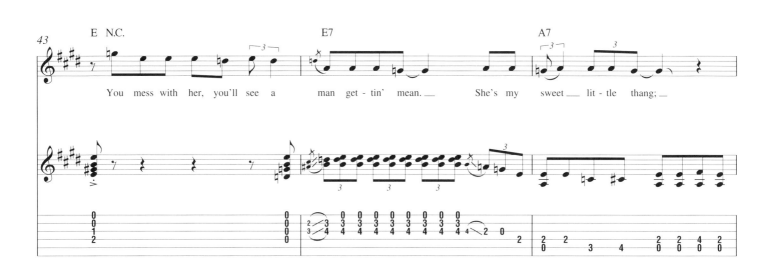

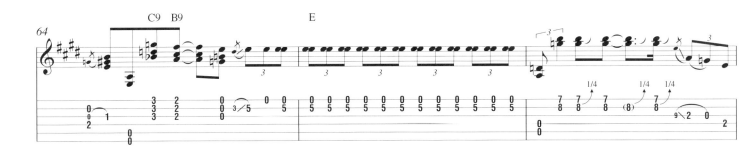

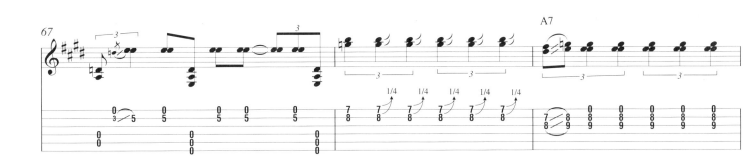

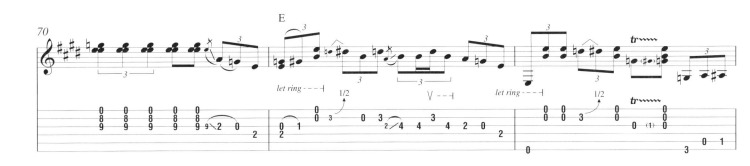

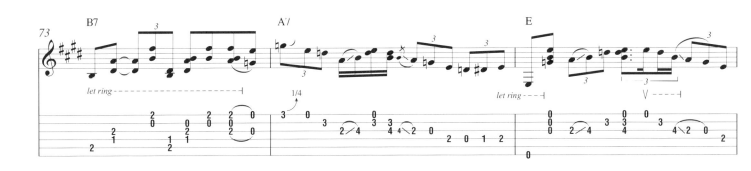

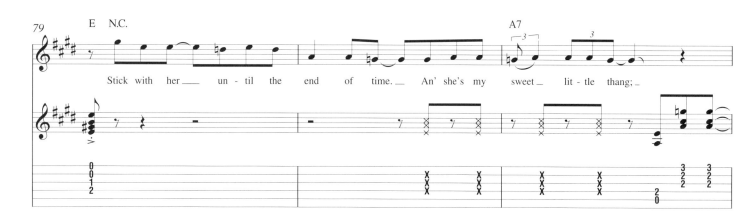

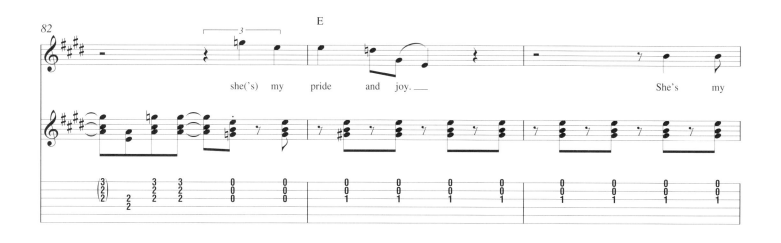

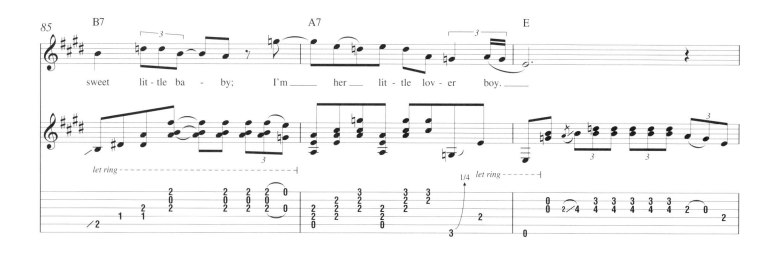

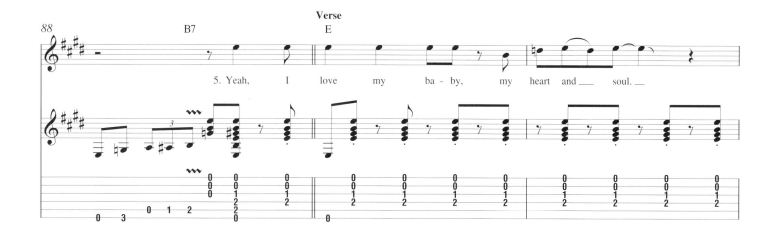

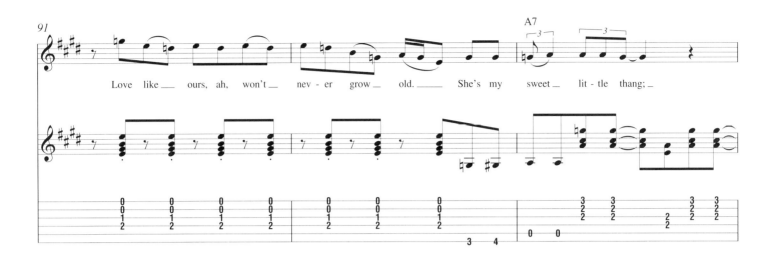

Love like — ours, ah, won't — nev-er grow — old. — She's my sweet — lit-tle thang; —

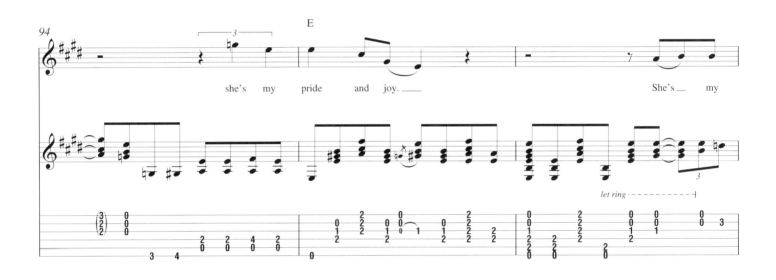

she's my pride and joy. — She's — my

sweet lit-tle ba- by; I'm — her — lit-tle lov-er boy. —

Guitar Solo

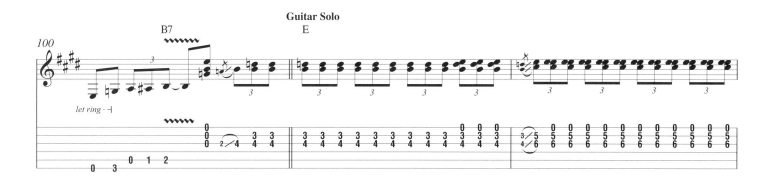

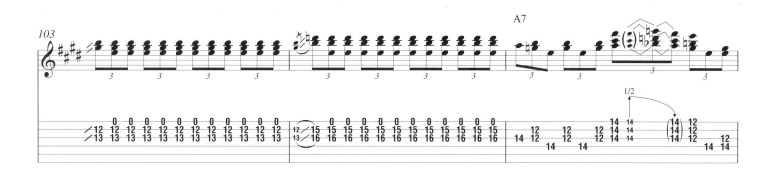

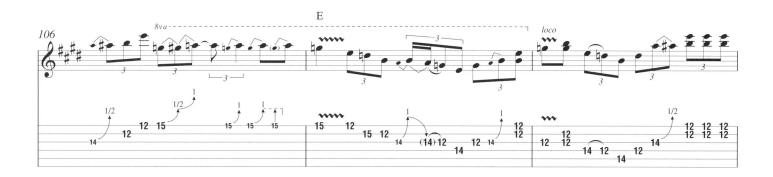

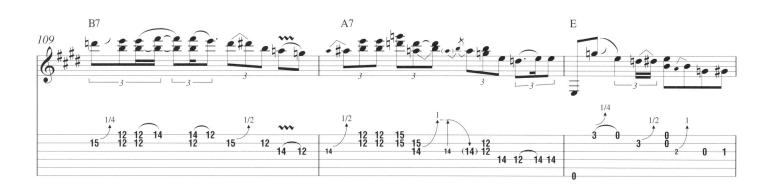

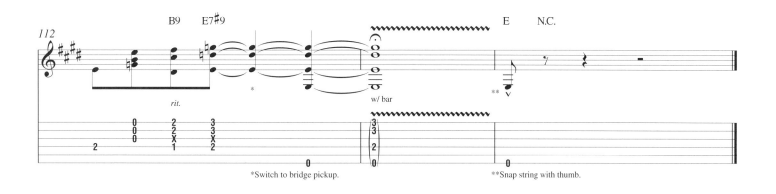

*Switch to bridge pickup. **Snap string with thumb.

Tightrope
From *In Step*, 1989

When Stevie cut what would sadly turn out to be his last studio effort, *In Step* (1989), he leaned on more of an R&B/soul approach than he ever had before, evidenced in particular by the hit tracks "Crossfire" and "Tightrope."

"Tightrope" is a straightforward 4/4 groove with a James Brown-meets-Stax type of feel. For the solo, SRV shifts gears by leaning on hard-swinging blues-infused lines, backed by able interplay from his Double Trouble band: Tommy Shannon (bass), Chris "Whipper" Layton (drums), and Reese Wynans (keyboards). The track was essentially cut live in the studio, encouraging the incredible synchronicity between the band members, especially Stevie and Chris. For reference, the song transcription begins on page 66.

Intro

The swinging feel of "Tightrope" can be described as straight 16ths played with a triplet feel, which means that two consecutive 16th notes are actually played as an eighth note and a 16th note within a triplet bracket, creating a stronger emphasis on the eighth-note downbeats and upbeats. If this sounds confusing, just think of it as a typical 12/8 blues shuffle feel, but played at a faster than normal tempo.

The "Tightrope" intro is based on the triadic chord tones of E major (E–G♯–B) and D major (D–F♯–A), followed by the chords B7, A, and E5; the main riff wraps up with a single-note line based on the E blues scale (E–G–A–B♭–B–D), played in open position.

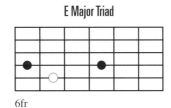

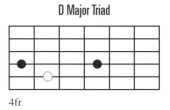

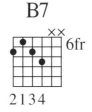

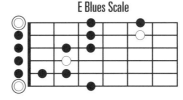

Throughout this intro section, the pick hand should maintain a steady down-up-down-up movement when executing straight or syncopated 16th-note rhythms. That way, the pick hand will stay locked into the groove and help to drive the beat of the song.

Verse

The verse section is driven by a funky 16th-note-based rhythm part that "sits" on a B7 chord. Though one could easily play the same one-bar rhythm throughout the verse and achieve an appropriately musical sound, SRV often mixes up the syncopation and adds random low-B bass notes to spice up his rhythm part.

Example 1 illustrates the basic one-bar rhythm, and then ventures into rhythmic embellishment along the lines of what Stevie would play in a live situation.

Tightrope
Example 1

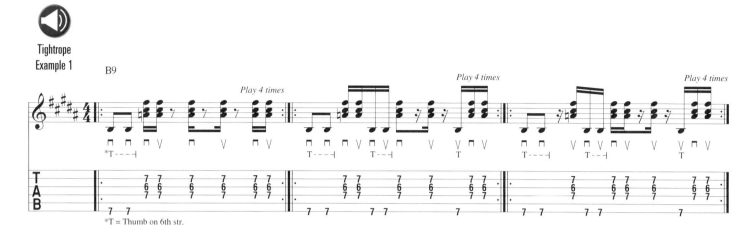

*T = Thumb on 6th str.

After brief G♯m and E9 chords, the intro riff is revisited to close out the verse section.

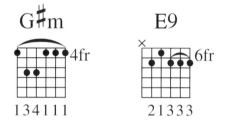

Chorus

Stevie applies the same 16th-note-driven funk-style rhythmic approach to the chorus chords as he did during the verse section, relying on the same rhythmic syncopation that serves to define the groove and feel of the song. He moves from E9 to B9 (see below), and after playing this alternating chord pattern three times, moves to A, E9, and B9, similar to the end of the verse section, but with A in place of G♯m.

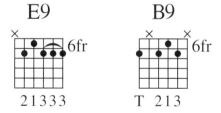

Example 2 illustrates the last two bars of the chorus section, which wraps up with a single-note riff based on B minor pentatonic (B–D–E–F♯–A) that functions as a springboard to the solo section.

Tightrope
Example 2

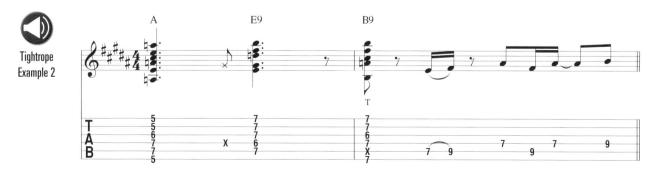

Guitar Solo

The solo section of this song consists of one standard 12-bar "blues" solo over the I–IV–V (B7–E7–F#7) progression in the key of B. His second solo chorus is played over the same progression for the first 10 bars, but he rounds out this chorus with a reprise of the intro lick, built from E and D major arpeggios, which transition to B7, A, and E5 chords.

SRV leans on but two scales throughout this entire solo: B minor pentatonic and B major pentatonic.

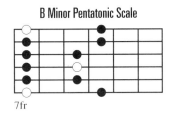

B Minor Pentatonic Scale

7fr

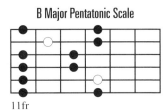

B Major Pentatonic Scale

11fr

Stylistically, one can clearly hear the B.B./Albert King influences, particularly the lick in bars 6–8 of the first chorus, illustrated in Example 3. Here, Albert King-style bends in 10th position give way to a slide down the fretboard back to seventh-position B minor pentatonic licks. One can also hear the Jimi Hendrix influence in the loose, relaxed feel with which Stevie executes these solo phrases.

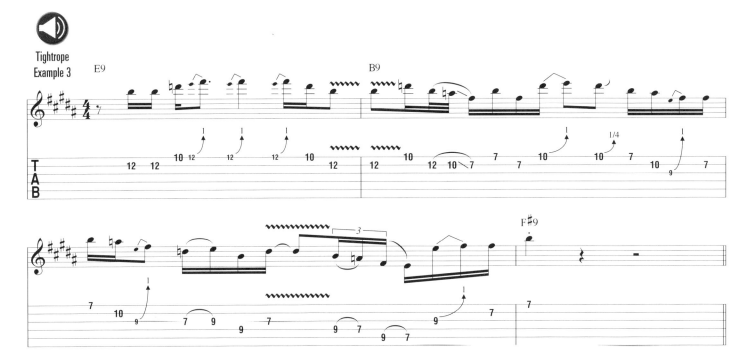

Tightrope
Example 3

Stevie ends his first solo chorus with a repetitive lick based on a "threes on fours" rhythmic approach that fills the last three bars of the section. Playing straight 16th notes, the shape of the riff is built from a repetitive three-note phrase, as shown in Example 4.

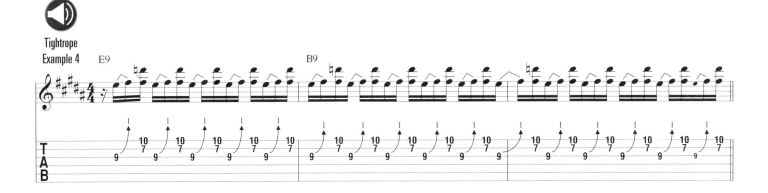

Tightrope
Example 4

SRV revisits this rhythmic approach during bar 9 of his second solo chorus, as shown in Example 5.

Tightrope
Example 5

Note that the notes choices in Example 5—E to F♯ to D—are exactly the same as those in Example 4, but Example 5 is played one octave lower.

Outro Guitar Solo

During bars 4–8 of the outro solo, SRV relies on a repetitive phrase that is articulated by bending a note on the second string up one whole step and catching the third string under the same fretting finger, bending the third string one half step (see photo). While holding these bends in place, heavy vibrato is applied. This technique, popularized by Jimi Hendrix, requires precise bending intonation, as well as substantial fret-hand strength.

Practice Example 6 to get a handle on this somewhat difficult to execute, but very expressive technique. Stevie revisits this technique in bars 15–17, shifting the concept to the top two strings.

Tightrope
Example 6

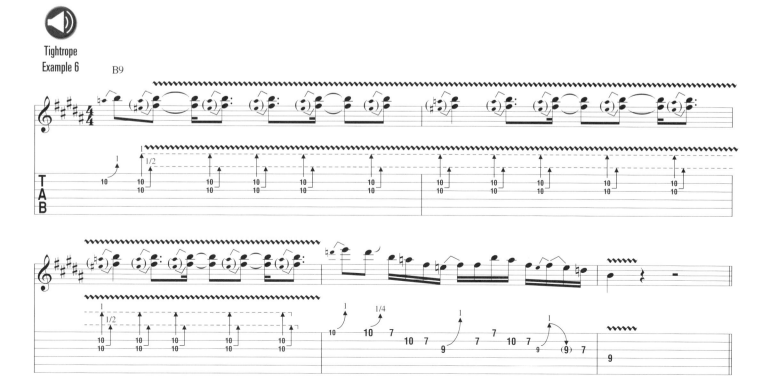

TIGHTROPE

Written by Stevie Ray Vaughan and Doyle Bramhall

Tightrope
Full Song

Tune down 1/2 step:
(low to high) Eb-Ab-Db-Gb-Bb-Eb

Intro

Moderately slow ♩ = 98

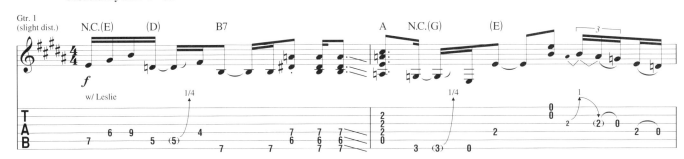

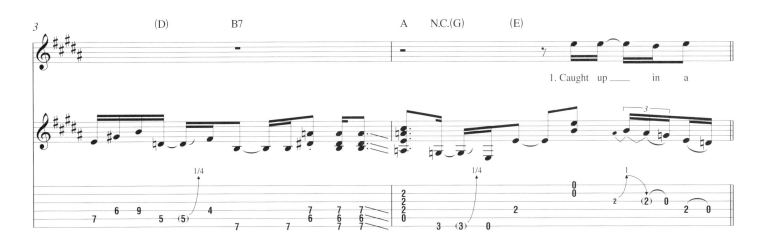

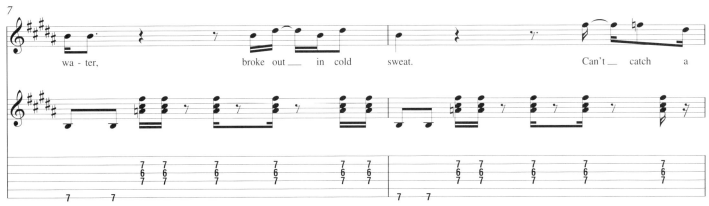

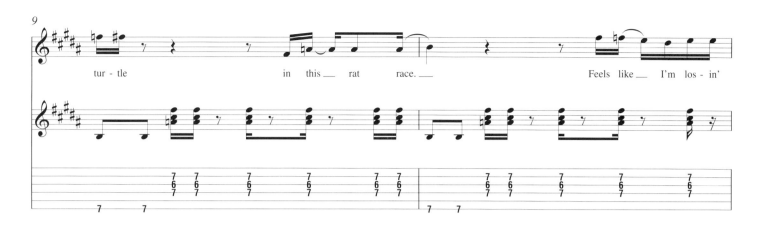

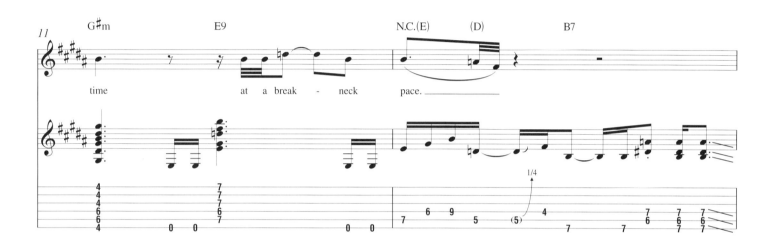

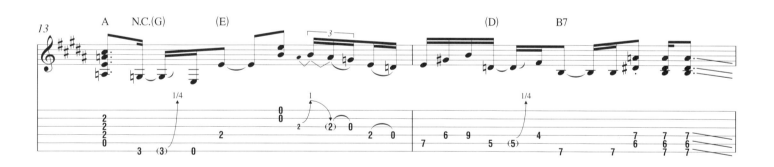

Verse

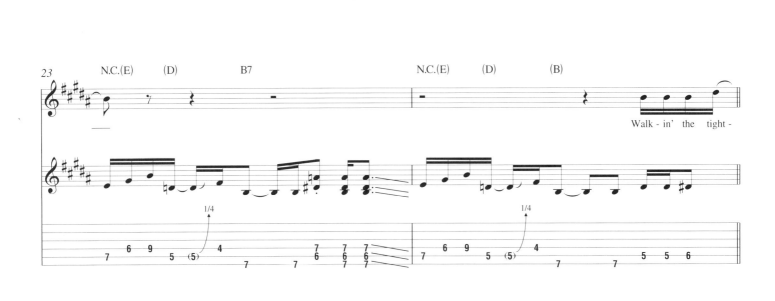

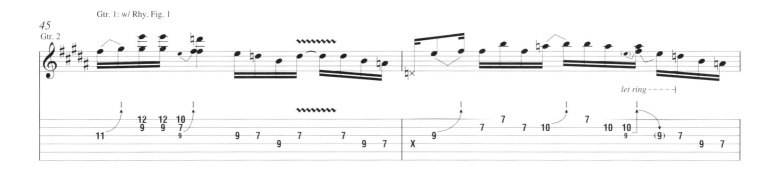

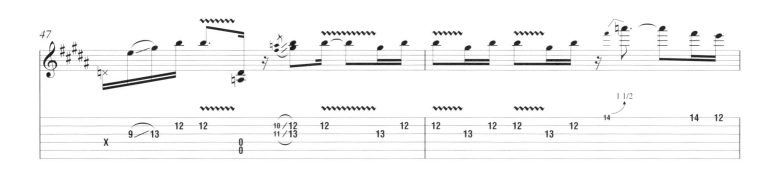

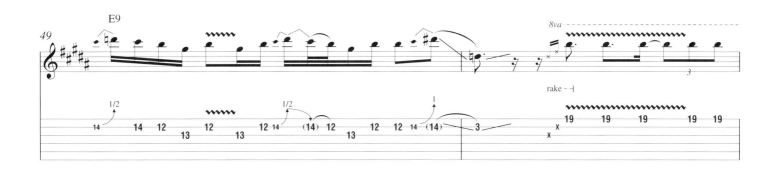

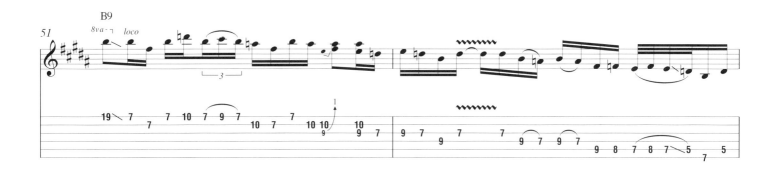

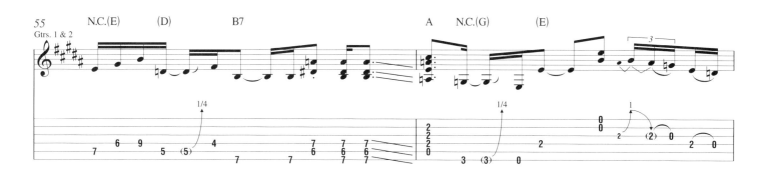

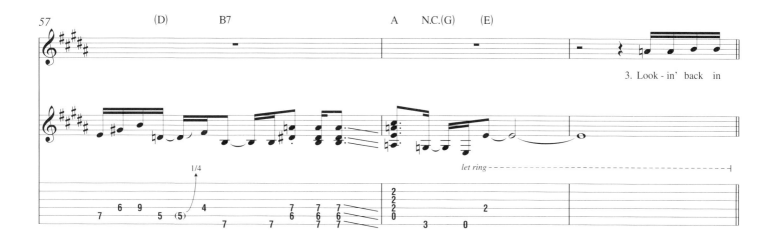

Verse

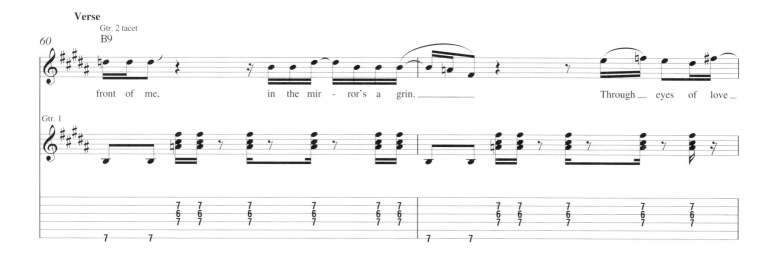

prob - lems.   That's the way __ life   is. __   My heart __ goes out to

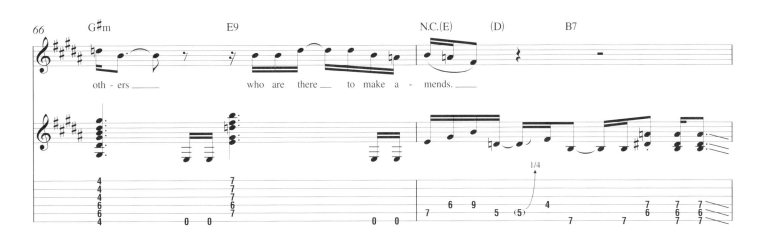

oth - ers __   who are there __ to make a - mends. __

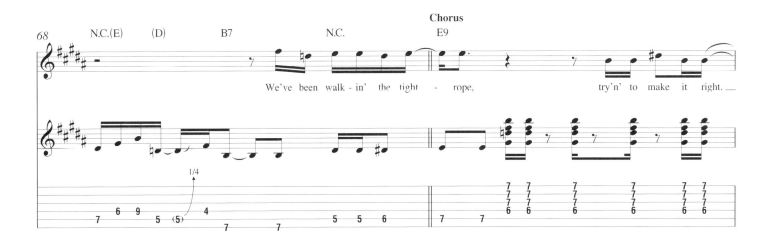

We've been walk - in' the tight - rope,   try'n' to make it right. __

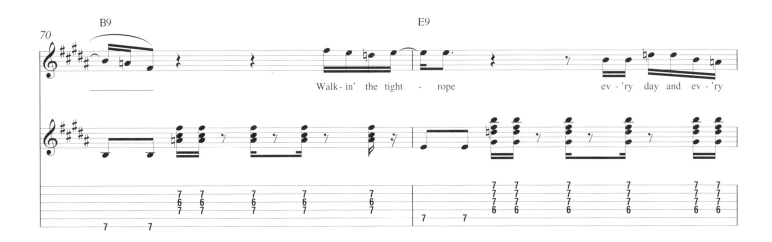

Walk - in' the tight - rope   ev - 'ry day and ev - 'ry

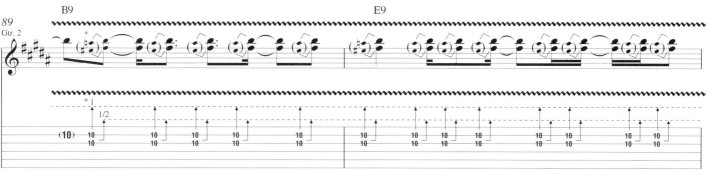

*Allow 3rd string to be caught under ring finger, next 5 meas.

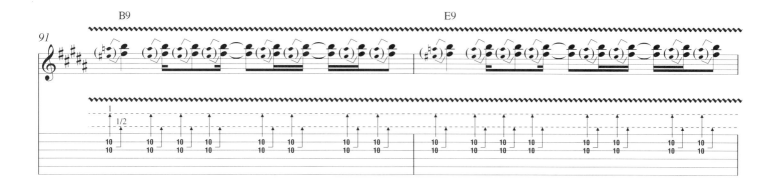

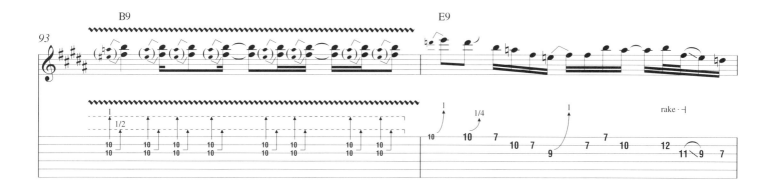

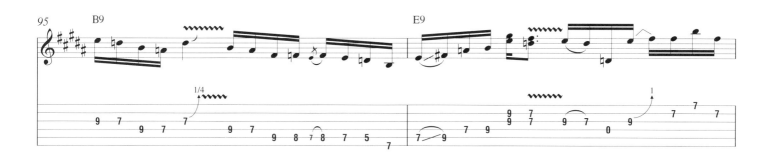

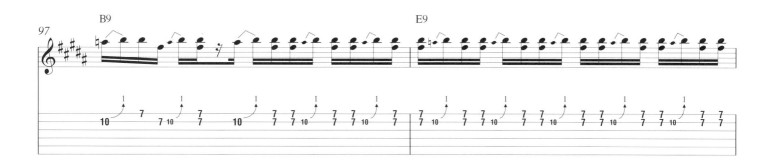

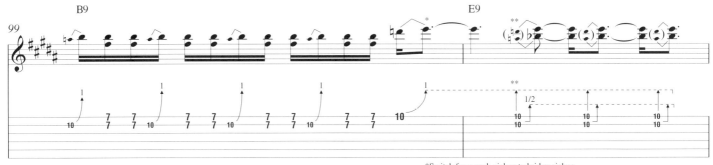

*Switch from neck pickup to bridge pickup.

**Allow 2nd string to be caught under ring finger, next 3 meas.

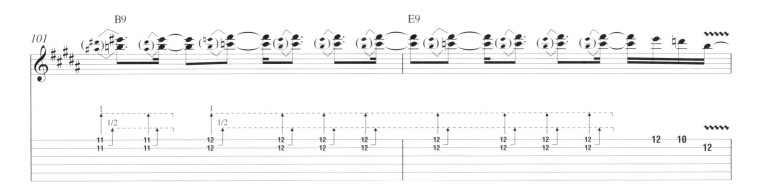

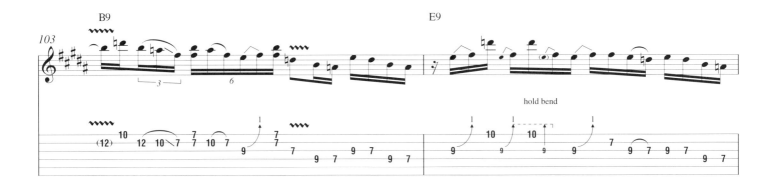

Begin fade

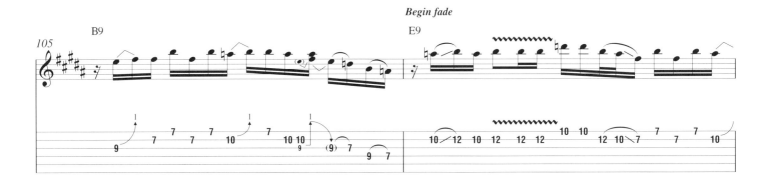

Fade out

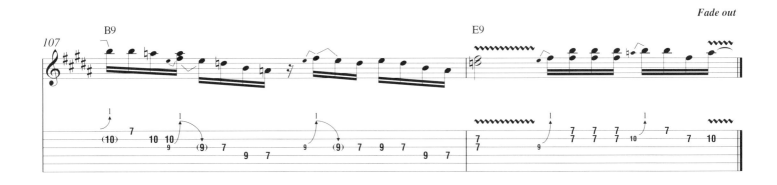

ESSENTIAL LICKS

Stevie Ray Vaughan's distinctive, one-of-a-kind guitar style is made up of a great many stylistic elements, all of which demonstrate his complete mastery of both rhythm and lead guitar techniques. In this section, we will address essential SRV licks that fall under both rhythm and lead guitar categories, with in-depth examination of the things that Stevie did to establish his unique and distinctive voice as a guitarist. Once you have a handle on all of these techniques within the context shown here, try applying them to as many different grooves and keys as you can in order to fully explore the potential of each expressive musical approach.

First and foremost, Stevie Ray Vaughan was a *blues* guitarist, and he had mastered all of the elements of the genre. The language of blues guitar is generally spoken with just a handful of scales: minor pentatonic, major pentatonic, and the blues scale, with bits of other scales and modes (Dorian, Mixolydian, Aeolian, etc.) thrown in. In order to truly master blues guitar, one must learn all of these scales in every key and in every fretboard position.

Open Position

Let's begin with the key and scales that SRV used most often: the key of E and the E minor pentatonic and E blues scales. If you look at the four studio albums that Stevie released in his lifetime, you'll find 18 songs recorded in the key of E, including some of his most well-known and oft-covered songs, such as "Pride and Joy," "Mary Had a Little Lamb," "Scuttle Buttin'," "Rude Mood," and "Riviera Paradise."

Two essential scale positions, one for E minor pentatonic and one for the E blues scale, are illustrated below. Be sure to memorize both of these scale patterns, with special attention paid to the location of all of the E root notes, which are indicated with open circles.

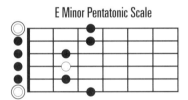

E Minor Pentatonic Scale

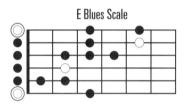

E Blues Scale

One of the primary reasons that guitarists enjoy playing in the key of E is the potential for incorporating all of the open strings into licks, riffs, or chords. When playing in E, SRV always leaned on the open-position E minor pentatonic and E blues scales for a great many licks.

Lick 1

This first lick illustrates an E minor pentatonic-based phrase that Stevie uses as his turnaround lick in bars 11–12 of the verse sections of "Pride and Joy." This lick, written in 4/4 time, is played with a triplet feel, which means that notes written as straight eighths should be articulated as a quarter note followed by an eighth note within a triplet bracket; therefore, instead of sounding evenly-spaced notes as one usually does when playing consecutive eighth notes, the eighth note indicated on each downbeat is held for the equivalent of the first two eighth notes of an eighth-note triplet, and the eighth note indicated on the upbeat is sounded as the last eighth note of an eighth-note triplet.

The lick begins with a four-note E major chord played on beat 1, followed by the top two strings played open and then a middle-finger slide up the G string from the second to the fourth fret. While holding this note, fret the D note at the third fret of the second string. Then, while holding both of these notes, sound the open high-E string. Next, while still fretting the two notes, drag the pick in an upward motion across the top three strings, moving from the first to the third string; this is known as a *reverse rake*. As soon as you strike the G string, slide the middle finger down to the second fret and then pull off to the open G string. This figure, and many of the licks that Stevie used in this style, can be heard in the playing of one of SRV's biggest influences, Lightnin' Hopkins.

Lick 1

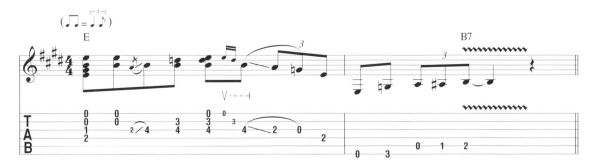

Lick 2

Here's another typical turnaround-style lick that SRV would pay on blues shuffles in the key of E, like "Pride and Joy." The two-note (B–D) figure played on the third and second strings is strummed repeatedly in eighth-note triplets, after which Stevie slides back down the G string in the same manner as Lick 1. In bar 2, after "walking" straight up the E blues scale, the figure ends with a second-inversion A triad (E–A–C♯) and a return to the I chord, represented by an E triad (E–G♯–B).

Lick 2

Lick 3

The best way to get licks like these under your fingers and into your muscle memory is to play them as repeated phrases: In bars 1–2, a slide up from A to B on the G string is followed by a three-note shape on the top three strings, which is sounded twice. This eighth-note triplet figure is executed on beats 1–3, followed by a slide back down the G string. Bar 2 replicates bar 1, and in bar 3, the opening phrase is played on all four beats. The lick then ends in bar 4, starting with a subtle quarter-step bend on G, followed by a gradual descent through the E minor pentatonic scale, ending with a *trill*—a fast, repetitive hammer-on/pull-off—between G and G♯.

Lick 3

Lick 4

The great majority of blues songs are played in major keys and the chord progressions feature dominant seventh chords. Though E minor pentatonic and the E blues scales are perfect for soloing over dominant chords, neither scale accurately "describes" a dominant seventh sound, because the chord tones of dominant seven are 1–3–5–♭7, and neither minor pentatonic nor the blues scale include the major 3rd. Most blues players either include the major 3rd in many of the licks that they play when soloing over dominant seventh chords, or will occasionally bend the minor 3rds up one half step in order to sound major 3rds.

Lick 4 illustrates the E blues scale with the major 3rd, G♯, added, played in descending fashion. Notice that the minor 3rd, G, is played first, followed by the major third, G♯. The "scale" is notated this way because it reflects the manner in which the major 3rd is most commonly incorporated into the blues scale when played in its descending form.

Lick 5

Here is the same scale—the E blues scale with the major 3rd, G♯, added—but played in ascending form. In this example, the minor 3rd, G, is played first, followed by the major 3rd, G♯. Experiment with playing both forms in ascending and descending manner, and listen to how the major 3rd "brightens" the sound and mood of the scale.

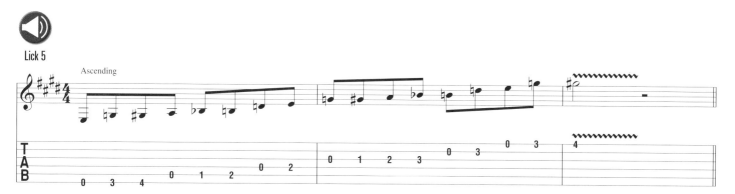

Lick 6

This lick offers an example of how SRV would often incorporate the major 3rd, G♯, into a phrase based primarily on the E blues scale, leaning on it here within a trill between G and G♯. In bar 2, the presence of the ♭7th, D, and the major 3rd, G♯, reflect the E7 tonality very clearly. You will hear Stevie play this exact lick, and licks very much like it, on E blues shuffles such as "I'm Crying," "Look at Little Sister," and "Pride and Joy."

When bending from the second fret of the G string, fret with the middle finger and line up the index finger directly behind the fretting finger in order to bolster the strength needed to bend with proper intonation. Stevie preferred very heavy string gauges, so if you prefer using these heavy gauges, you will have to build up proper strength in the fret hand.

Lick 7

Here is another good example of executing bends from the second fret of the G string. In this lick, along the lines of what Stevie plays on his cover version of Jimi Hendrix's "Voodoo Chile (Slight Return)," the middle finger of the fret hand is used to bend, release, and then pull off from the second fret of the G string. After sounding the whole-step bend, release the bend and then immediately pull off to the open G string, followed by E (fourth string, second fret). Stevie picks this figure very hard, so when the E note is sounded, the open B string often sounds simultaneously, as shown here.

Lick 7

Lick 8

Here's another example of how SRV would typically move through E minor pentatonic and the E blues scale when playing in open position and utilizing open strings. The majority of the phrase is based on steady eighth-note triplets, but on beat 3 of bar 2, a 16th-note subdivision is used to sound the *reverse rake* across the top three strings. This subtle change in rhythm adds a lot to the flavor of the lick, sharpening its intensity and providing extra push to the rhythm.

Lick 8

Lick 9

There are many examples of SRV using the shapes and melodic patterns shown in Licks 1–8 and "cramming" them into single beats or pairs of beats, resulting in 16th-note triplets and 32nd-note runs. This lick is along the lines of what he plays just before jumping into his "Voodoo Chile" solo: a quick, three-note figure that includes a pull-off from D (second string, third fret) to the open B string, followed by a rapid bend/release/pull-off on the G string as the phrase moves down to the E root note (fourth string, second fret). On beat 3, a quick hammer/pull is executed between the 4th, A, and the ♭5th, B♭, leading to the subtle quarter-step bend of the low G, followed by the open low-E and a hammer-on to the E one octave higher.

Lick 10

Now that you have a handle on the manner in which SRV would incorporate open strings when playing in the key of E, let's take a look at a lick that he plays in his first "Voodoo Chile" solo. Sticking with the top three strings, the open B and high E are quickly alternated with notes fretted on the third fret of the B string and the second fret of the G string. On beat 3, notice the incorporation of F♯, the 9th (also known as the major 2nd); this is a technique that Stevie loved and included in many of his solos. The phrase ends with a whole-step bend from D to E. Apply the necessary fret-hand strength in order to properly intonate this bend/vibrato.

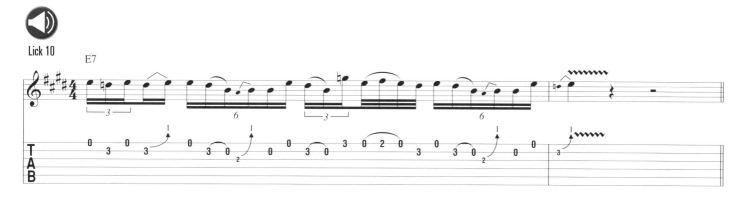

Lick 11

Let's explore further the inclusion of the major 2nd (9th) within the E blues scale. This lick shows the notes of the E blues scale played in descending manner with the major 2nd, F♯, added. Play this scale up and down repeatedly in order to memorize it. You will find a great many examples of Stevie incorporating the major 2nd into blues scale phrases, which we'll explore up and down the fretboard and in different keys in the upcoming licks.

Lick 12

Now let's try incorporating both the major 2nd and the major 3rd into E blues scale-style phrases. This lick, articulated in steady eighth-note triplets, features many of the same quick hammer-on/pull-off/slide figures that were used in the previous licks, but the presence of the major 2nd and major 3rd within the blues scale *environment* creates a more complex and interesting harmonic picture.

Lick 12

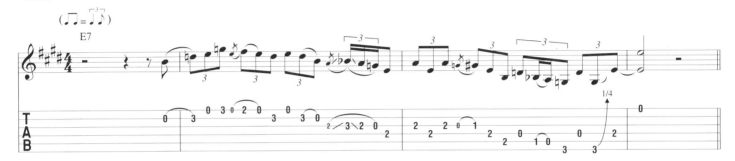

Lick 13

All blues and rock guitarists lean on repetitive phrases, or "cycled" licks, when performing improvised solos. Although elements such as these might not be true improvisation, as the parts have been practiced extensively, cycled licks are the way by which guitarists (and soloists of all genres and instruments) learn to "speak the language" of the music that they choose to perform.

This lick is based on a repetitive eighth-note triplet wherein the first note features a whole-step bend from A to B on the G string, followed by the open B and high-E strings. Play this one-beat phrase on each beat, in a repetitive manner.

Lick 13

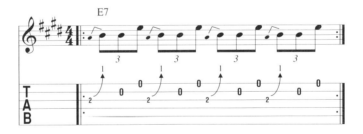

Lick 14

Here is another commonly used eighth-note triplet lick that is repeated on each beat. The phrase starts with a subtle quarter-step bend on G (first string, third fret), followed by the open high-E and B strings. Practice this phrase over and over until it flows with the proper "rolling" feeling.

Lick 14

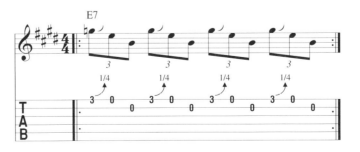

Lick 15

Here's the third of three eighth-note triplet phrases whose notes are repeated on each beat of the bar. Starting with an eighth-note pickup, the open B string is followed by a hammer-on to the D note at the third fret and the open high-E and B strings, which begin the cycle again. Practice all three of these licks repeatedly and in succession in order to compare them and to get the feeling of executing these shapes under your fingers.

Lick 15

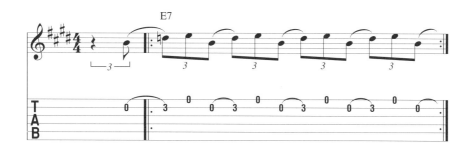

Lick 16

Now that you have all three of these licks memorized, let's try combining them into a longer cycled phrase. In this lick, a note is fretted on every downbeat as we move from the G string to the B and high-E strings and then back to the G string. Playing these shapes in this sequence sounds much more musical than when each is played individually, over and over. Play through this lick at a slow tempo, gradually increasing the speed until you are able to execute the longer phrase smoothly and effortlessly. This will come in very handy when tackling some of the more complex SRV licks to follow.

Lick 16

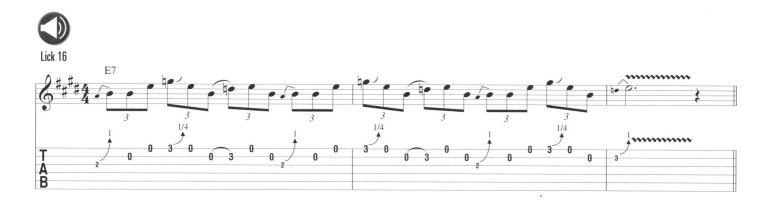

Lick 17

Stevie often moved this concept (i.e., cycled licks) from the high strings to the low strings; a great example can be heard in his approach to the long solos that he played in the slow and meditative "Lenny." In this lick, also played as a steady succession of eighth-note triplets, B♭ is pulled off to the open A, followed by a low G.

Lick 17

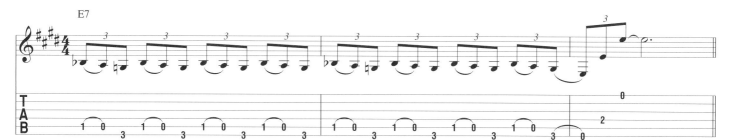

Lick 18

A slight twist to the previous lick can be provided by simply beginning with an open-A grace note, which is hammered onto B♭, followed by a pull-off back to the open A and then the low G note. Once again, start slowly and gradually build up speed in order to execute these phrases with the rapidity and effortlessly smooth quality so often demonstrated by Stevie.

Lick 18

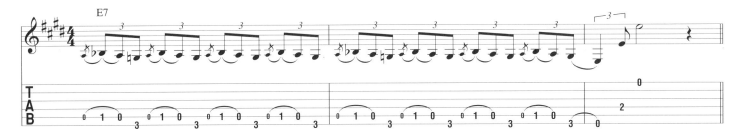

Lick 19

In this lick, Stevie alternates between moving downward and moving upward within the phrase, performing a pattern that is three beats in length but played in straight 4/4 time, creating what is known as a "threes on fours" concept. Fret all notes with either the index or middle finger and strive for clarity and smooth execution.

Lick 19

Lick 20

Another great trick is to add the ♭9th, which is an F note in the key of E. This lick offers an SRV-style example of incorporating the ♭9th into eighth-note triplet style phrases, wrapping up with the inclusion of G♯, the major 3rd, in order to strengthen the lick's connection to the dominant seventh (E7) sound.

Lick 20

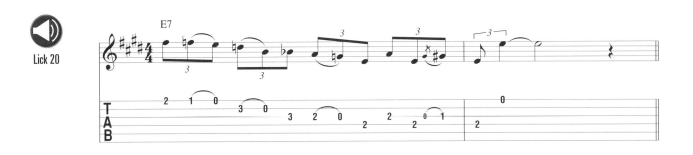

Lick 21

Great licks are most often created by combining small melodic phrases into one long musical statement, and this lick offers an excellent example in that it is built from the combination of the last group of licks that we examined. Close study of Stevie Ray's playing reveals that he very often relied on the same (or very similar) licks and phrases but drew from the "musicality" of the moment to convey inspired performances in his solos.

Lick 21

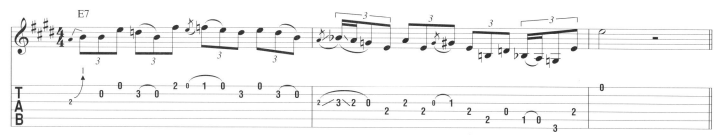

Closed Positions

Now that you have a firm grasp of SRV's soloing approach in regard to his use of minor pentatonic, the blues scale, and the inclusion of other "passing tones," let's move these phrases up one octave (to 12th position), translating these open-string licks to closed-position licks that can be played in any key, anywhere on the fretboard.

The first thing to do is to examine E minor pentatonic and the E blues scale as it falls in 12th position, illustrated in the accompanying diagrams. Notice that the patterns are exactly the same as when playing in open position, but now you must use the index finger to fret all notes located at the 12th fret. When playing in this position (or any closed "box" patterns of minor pentatonic and the blues scale), Stevie most often used the middle finger for notes fretted two frets higher than the index finger on the G string, and used the ring finger for notes fretted three frets higher on the B string. Play these patterns up and down repeatedly in order to memorize them and work them into your muscle memory.

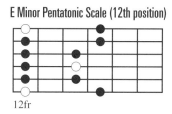

E Minor Pentatonic Scale (12th position)

12fr

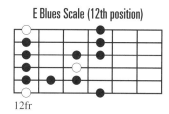

E Blues Scale (12th position)

12fr

Lick 22

Along with these "box" patterns (scale patterns that stay in a single fretboard position), it is essential to become acquainted with extended scale patterns of both E minor pentatonic and the E blues scale. Lick 22 illustrates an extended pattern of the E minor pentatonic scale that starts at the 10th fret and gradually moves up the fretboard to the 19th fret.

Lick 22

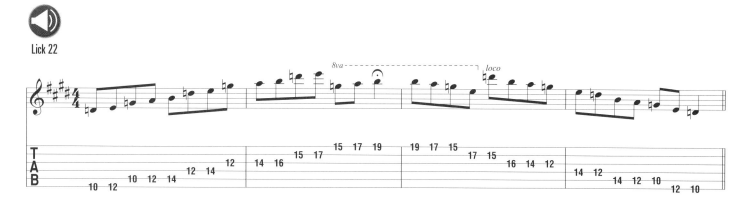

Lick 23

Once you have this extended scale position of E minor pentatonic memorized, simply add the ♭5th (flatted 5th), B♭, to convert it to the extended E blues scale, as shown below. Once again, practice this extended scale pattern in ascending and descending form until it is firmly under your fingers.

Lick 23

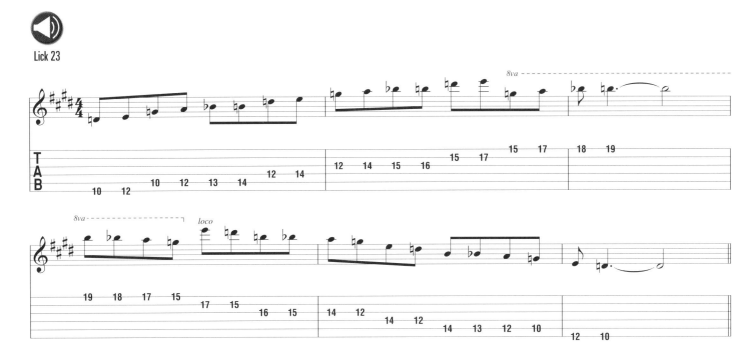

Lick 24

Stevie begins his "Voodoo Chile" solo with E minor pentatonic licks played in 12th position (as does Jimi Hendrix on the song's original studio recording). This lick represents the first four bars of Stevie's solo; notice how he moves through his melodic lines in an effortless manner, all the while staying firmly rooted in 12th position. Bars 1–2 both feature a handful of *pre-bends*, wherein a string is bent a specific distance before it is sounded: in bar 1, on the last 16th note of beat 1 and on the first 16th note of beat 2, D is pre-bent one whole step to E before it is struck; in bar 2, A is pre-bent one whole step to B but is then gradually *unbent* while striking the string repeatedly. Another essential technique is the use of *bent vibrato*, heard on the last note in bar 1. While holding a pre-bent D (up one whole step to E), apply fret-hand vibrato by holding the fret-hand and wrist firmly and shaking the forearm. There will be a complete study of SRV's vibrato techniques later in the book.

Lick 24

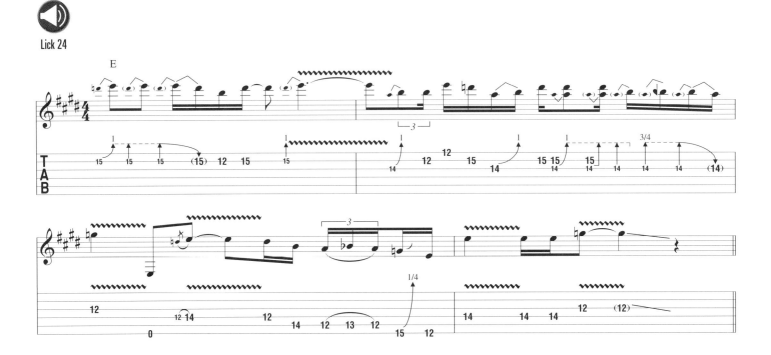

Lick 25

This lick, taken from Stevie's first solo on "Pride and Joy," offers a slight twist on the E minor and E blues scales, as SRV uses *double stops* (two-note shapes) that are separated by 3rds on the G and B strings, played in conjunction with the open high-E string. The major 3rd and 5th, G♯ and B, sounded in bar 1, slide up three frets in bar 2 to sound B and D, the 5th and ♭7th. In bar 4, the index finger is used to barre across the top two strings at the 12th fret while notes are bent up one half step (G string) and one quarter step (B string).

Lick 25

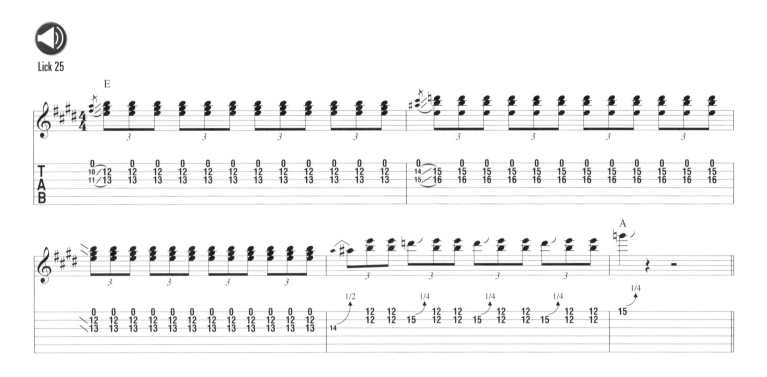

Lick 26

Stevie reprises the approach used in Lick 25 at the beginning of his "Pride and Joy" outro solo, as shown below. The double-stop figure here begins in third position and then gradually moves up the fretboard to fifth, 12th, and 15th position before the lick shifts back down to the 12th-position E minor pentatonic scale pattern.

Lick 26

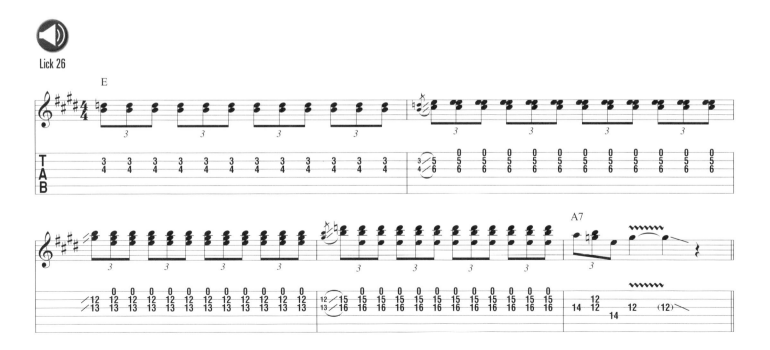

Lick 27

A technique Stevie often employed was the dramatic and sudden shift from one scale position to the position either one octave higher or one octave lower. This lick, heard during his "Honey Bee" solo, begins with the extended higher position of E minor pentatonic, but in bar 3, there is a very sudden shift down to open position, which serves to add power and intensity to the solo phrase.

Lick 28

This lick represents the four-bar phrase that kicks off Stevie's "Look at Little Sister" solo. The first three bars remain rooted in 12th position, for which he keeps the fret-hand index finger barred across the top two strings at the 12th fret while alternating whole-, half-, and quarter-step bends between strings 3–1. Notice his use of steady eighth-note triplets, which drive the rhythm of the song forward. In bar 4, he gradually slides up the high E string, moving to 15th and then 17th position and altering the phrasing of the triplet rhythm in the process.

Lick 29

Now let's take these eighth-note triplet phrases and recreate them within 16th-note triplet phrases, as SRV does so often when playing either on a slow blues or any relatively slow tempo tune. This lick, taken from the studio recording of his "Little Wing" solo, is built from many of the same shapes and patterns found in previous licks, but they are now executed as 16th-note triplets against a slow tempo in 4/4 time. Strive for both rhythmic precision and clear articulation, both essential earmarks of SRV's distinct style.

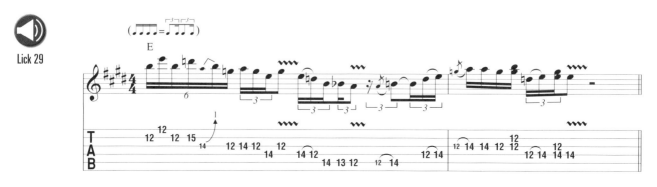

Lick 30

"Voodoo Chile" offers more great examples of how SRV incorporates melodic shapes and patterns into phrases built from a steady progression of 16th-note triplets. Once again, the fret hand remains rooted in 12th position throughout, and you should strive for correct intonation when string bending. In bar 1, on the upbeat of beat 4, a fast hammer/pull is executed on the high E string immediately after fretting a high G note (15th fret). Use the ring finger to fret the G note and the middle finger to fret the F♯ (14th fret).

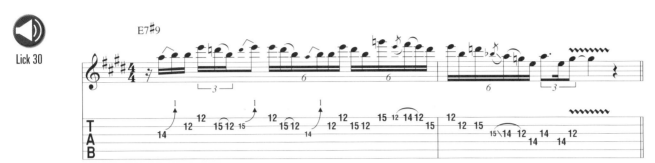

Lick 31

We can also place these types of phrases within the context of a fast tempo solo, resulting in lines written primarily as eighth and 16th notes. A perfect example can be found in the soloing that Stevie performs on the uptempo song "Testify." This lick, derived from his first solo, remains rooted in 12th position and SRV sticks with a three-finger approach: notes at the 12th fret are fretted with the index finger, notes at the 14th fret are fretted with the middle finger, and notes at the 15th fret are fretted with the ring finger. When moving to the wound strings, SRV would often switch from the middle to the ring finger, so notes fretted at the 14th fret of the D or A string would oftentimes be alternately fretted with the ring finger.

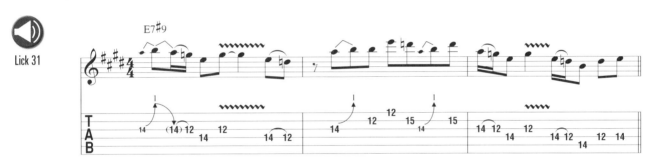

A large measure of Stevie's brilliance lays in his impeccable technique, honed from years and years of intense dedication to perfecting his craft. Stevie's complete mastery of the licks shown thus far enabled him to easily turn on a dime within the split-second spontaneity of a guitar solo. Practicing his favorite licks and phrases in every key and within every fretboard position was an obsession of his, so let's likewise move the prior closed-position phrases to other keys and other areas of the fretboard.

A perfect place to start is the key of G, as played in third position. Stevie played a variety of tunes in this key, such as "Texas Flood" and "The Things (That) I Used to Do," and always demonstrated absolute fluidity, power, and speed when improvising in this position. Examine the scale patterns shown for G minor pentatonic, the G blues scale, and the extended pattern of the G blues scale, as all of these will be put to use in the next handful of licks.

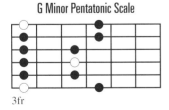

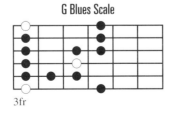

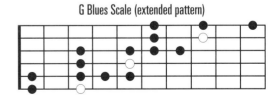

Lick 32

Just as we had done with the open-position E minor pentatonic pattern, it's essential to master some basic lick shapes in G minor pentatonic. This first lick is built from a one-beat phrase played in an eighth-note triplet rhythm: use the ring and/or middle finger to execute the whole-step bend on the G string, and use the index finger to barre across the top two strings at the third fret. Additionally, use a down-down-up picking pattern throughout the bar.

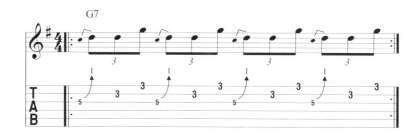

Lick 33

This next essential eighth-note triplet figure also features the bend as the first note, this time located on the high E string and executed as a half-step bend, followed by G and D on the top two strings, both fretted with an index-finger barre. Use a down-up-down picking motion for this repetitive triplet figure.

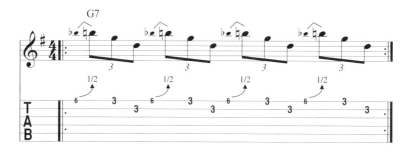

Lick 34

This lick represents a third essential eighth-note triplet shape for playing single-note lines in third position of G minor pentatonic or the G blues scale. To fret this lick as Stevie did, begin with the index finger on D (second string, third fret) and then hammer onto the F note at the sixth fret with the ring finger, followed by an index-finger barre for the high G (the barre also frets the second D, which facilitates "cycling" the lick many times over). One can also substitute the pinky for the ring finger if it feels more natural.

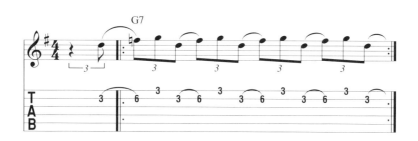

Lick 35

Now let's put the three essential pieces together into a unified lick, one that reflects the manner in which SRV would very often combine these types of eighth-note triplet shapes. Begin with the whole-step ring-finger bend from C to D on the G string, followed by the index-finger barre across the top two strings. Next, use the ring finger to fret the half-step bend on the high E string, and then also use the ring finger to hammer from D to F on the downbeat of beat 3. The cycle restarts on beat 4 with a repeat of the initial shape, so now the three-beat lick starts on beat 4 and is played through beats 1–2 of bar 2. When played as a repetitive two-bar lick (as it is here), the sequence of the shapes is "rearranged" when you revert back to the beginning of bar 1.

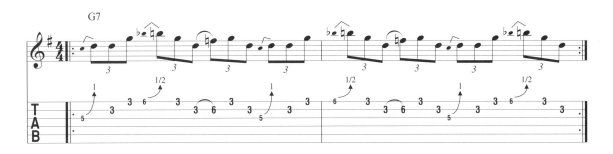

Lick 36

SRV always relied upon figures like Licks 32–35 when weaving solo lines over a slow blues, and this lick offers an example of how he might go about placing these shapes within that specific context. The previous eighth-note triplet shapes are played here as 16th-note triplets, in a slow 12/8 meter. Through beats 1–2, the shapes are sequenced just as they are in Lick 35, but on beat 3, the phrase wraps up with a slide/pull-off on the G string, followed by a G root note and a heavily vibratoed B♭ (minor 3rd).

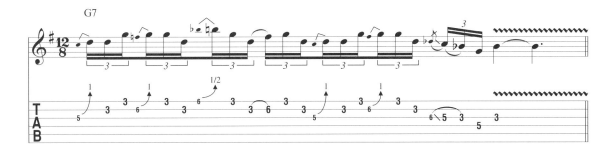

Lick 37

A sound that has become synonymous with the SRV signature approach is the inclusion of the 9th and ♭9th within the standard "box" pattern of the minor pentatonic scale. This lick, also played in the key of G, can be heard on slow-blues tracks like "Texas Flood" and "The Things (That) I Used to Do." It begins with a pickup B♭ that is hammered onto B, the major 3rd of G, followed by an index-finger barre across the top two strings, a subtle bend on F (second string, sixth fret), and the inclusion of A, the 9th, and a quick hammer/pull between G and A♭, the ♭9th. On beat 2, the quick hammer/pull on the high E string is expanded by one fret, moving between G and A, the 9th. At the very end of the phrase, a whole-step bend on the G string is followed by the G root note on the high E string and a jump back down to the G string to sound a heavily vibratoed B♭, emulating the great Albert King.

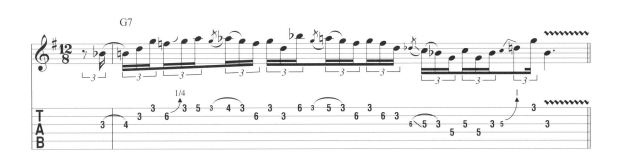

Lick 38

Further emulation of Albert King is illustrated in this lick with lines that are focused on the top part of the extended pattern of the G blues scale. Using the middle or ring finger of the pick hand to fingerpick, snap the high E string against the fretboard when sounding all of the notes on that string. Notice the somewhat unusual half-step bend from the major 3rd, B, to the 4th, C, which is then bent an additional whole step to D, executed as a one-and-a-half-step "overbend." When moving into beat 4, the index finger shifts from the sixth fret of the B string to the fifth fret of the G string before articulating the whole-step bend/release/slide down to the third fret.

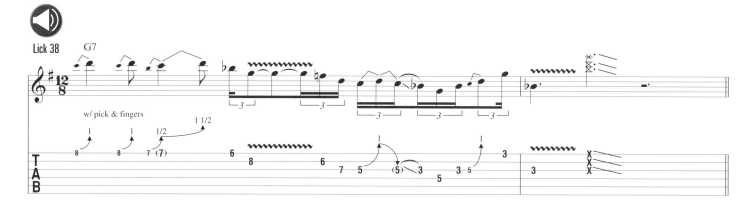

One of the absolute true staples of blues soloing involves the incorporation of what has become affectionately known as the "B.B. box," so named for blues guitar great B.B. King. This very specific fretboard position facilitates certain blues phrases that every aspiring blues guitarist should have in their arsenal. Study the accompanying box pattern and, once memorized, move on to the lick examples. The unique character of this box pattern is due to the manner in which it combines elements of major pentatonic, minor pentatonic, and the blues scale.

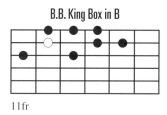

B.B. King Box in B

11fr

Lick 39

This lick comes from SRV's second solo chorus in the song "Tightrope," at the point at which he switches from B minor pentatonic to lines based primarily on B major pentatonic as it relates to the "B.B. box." Notice how Stevie repeatedly accentuates the major sixth, G♯, alternating this interval with higher B root note. He also moves from a one-and-a-half-step overbend—F♯ to A on the high E string—to more subtle half-step bends from C♯ to D on the B string.

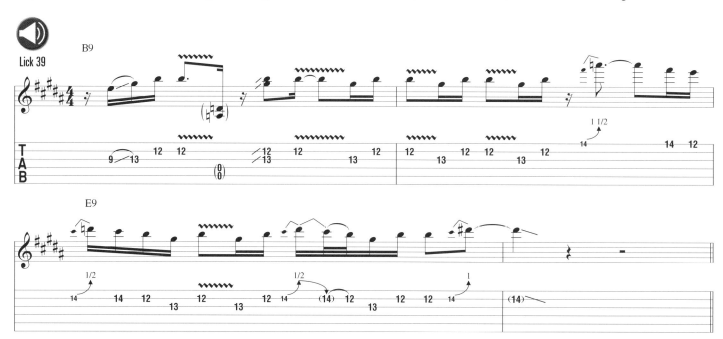

One of Stevie Ray Vaughan's absolute greatest performances is one that is somewhat obscure (though it is very well-known and loved by ardent fans)—his television studio performance with Albert King that was eventually released in 2010 as a DVD/CD under the title *In Session*. On the smoldering slow blues "Blues at Sunrise," SRV dips into the B.B. barrel towards the end of the tune, using the "B.B. box" in the key of G.

B.B. King Box in G

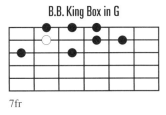

7fr

Lick 40

This two-bar phrase represents a bit of SRV's use of the "B.B. box" on "Blues at Sunrise." Here, he begins by moving dramatically from a C-to-D bend to a D-to-F bend on the high E string. This upward shift puts him in perfect position to play the subsequent fast phrases that are based within the "B.B. box" pattern. This is a fast, tricky lick, so play through it slowly and carefully, and listen to the recording as well. Strive for the precision and clarity that Stevie achieves so effortlessly.

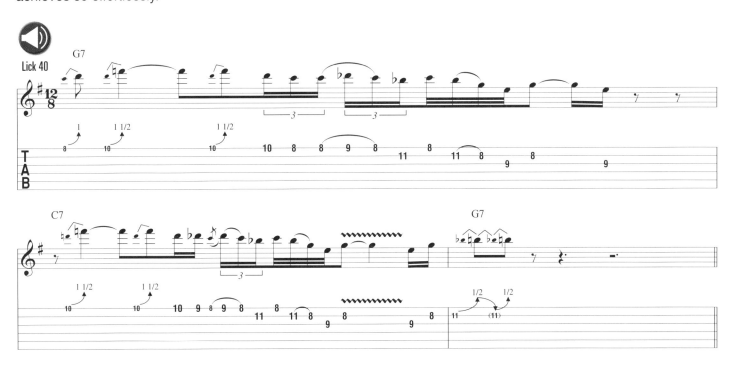

There are two more scales and scale patterns that are essential to a full understanding of SRV's soloing style: E major pentatonic (plus a version of E major pentatonic that includes passing tones) and a "hybrid" scale that combines elements of the blues scale and the Dorian mode.

First up is major pentatonic, illustrated in the key of E in the accompanying boxes. The first box illustrates the "basic" extended scale pattern, and the second box includes the ♭3rd and ♭6th passing tones. Play through both of these box positions, memorize them, and then move/transpose them to as many other keys as possible.

E Major Pentatonic Scale

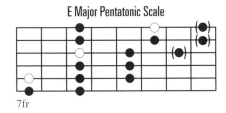

7fr

E Major Pentatonic Scale w/ ♭3 and ♭6

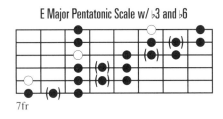

7fr

Lick 41

During the intro to the barn-burning "Rude Mood," recorded for his debut, *Texas Flood*, SRV jumps up the fretboard to play a fast E major pentatonic lick that begins in ninth position and then slides down to seventh position at the very end. Use the ring and index fingers to fret all of the notes in this lick, and take note of the subtle inclusion of pull-offs and slides, which are used to evoke a *legato* (smooth and connected) sound.

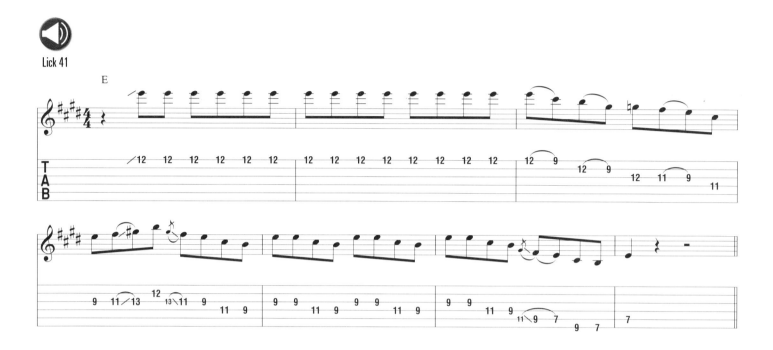

Lick 42

Stevie relies on E major pentatonic for much of the soloing in his original composition "Lenny" as well, as evidenced by this lick from his second solo. Moving primarily between the index and ring fingers, notice the very smooth and quick positional shifts, moving first from seventh to ninth position and then all the way down to fifth position. His deft use of legato techniques like hammer-ons, pull-offs, and slides aptly demonstrate his immaculate technique. Be sure to check out the mind-boggling live version of "Lenny" found on the *Live at El Mocambo* DVD.

The aforementioned "hybrid" scale—illustrated in the accompanying box as a combination of the A blues scale (A–C–D–E♭–E–G) and the A Dorian mode (A–B–C–D–E–F♯–G)—reveals the influence of T-Bone Walker and his disciple, Chuck Berry, on SRV, as Stevie relies on this "scale" for much of his soloing on tracks like "Love Struck Baby."

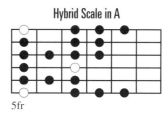

Hybrid Scale in A

5fr

Lick 43

This phrase is derived from Stevie's first solo on "Love Struck Baby." It begins with partial barres across the top two strings: for notes fretted on the eighth and seventh frets, use a ring-finger barre; for notes fretted at the fifth fret, use an index-finger barre. When playing through these phrases, it's helpful to keep the fret hand on a bit of a *diagonal*, as this will facilitate dragging the ring finger down the fretboard from the eighth to the seventh fret. Substantial fret-hand strength is also required to execute the repeated whole-step bends on the G string, so as usual, work on these phrases slowly and carefully and strive for clear articulation of each and every note.

Lick 43

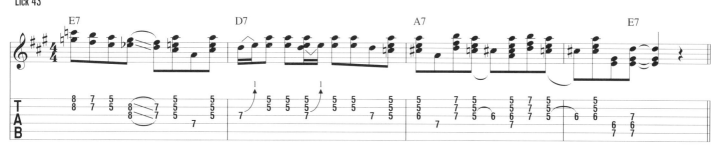

ESSENTIAL RIFFS

Ain't Gone 'N' Give Up on Love
From *Soul to Soul*, 1985

Originally cut for *Soul to Soul* (1985), "Ain't Gone 'N' Give Up on Love" is a slow-burning and emotive slow blues played in the key of A, delivered in inimitable SRV and Double Trouble style—powerful yet performed with laser-sharp dynamics. Joining the four-piece band on this track is brother Jimmie Vaughan on subtle but very effective rhythm guitar, treated with a rotating-speaker effect. There are also some interesting twists and turns found in the bridge chord progression. Throughout the song, Stevie's soloing style leans heavily on his Albert King influence, blended masterfully with his incredibly precise articulation and powerfully emotional execution.

Illustrated below is the intro of the song, during which Stevie performs exquisitely precise single-note blues lines in the style of his primary inspiration, Albert King. The accompanying diagram illustrates the fifth-fret A hybrid scale pattern that Stevie relies on for additional solo phrases.

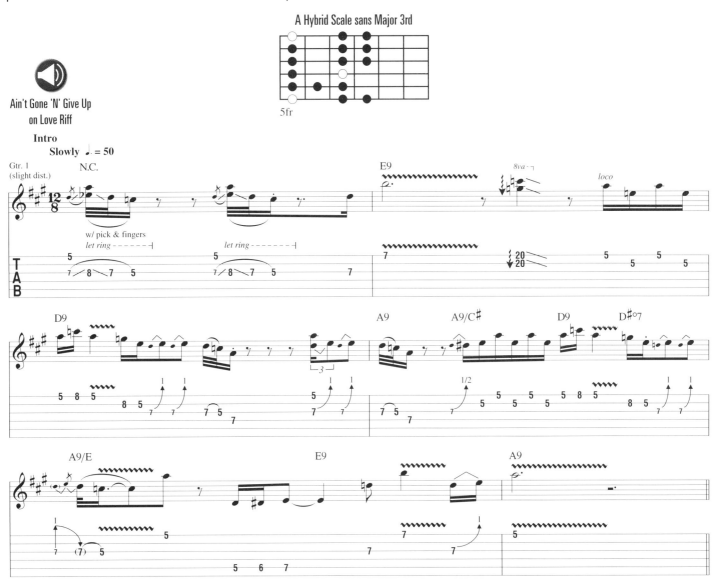

This excerpt begins with a pickup measure, which comes in on beat 3: the ring finger is used to quickly slide up and down on the G string, between the seventh and eighth frets (the 4th, D, and the ♭5th, E♭), while the index finger simultaneously frets a high A at the fifth fret of the high E string. This initial figure is hybrid-picked: held between the index finger and thumb, the pick is used to strike the G string while the pick-hand middle finger is used to fingerpick the high E string. The next bar represents bar 1 of the intro, which starts on the V chord, E9, played for one bar, followed by the IV chord, D9, also played for one bar, and the I–IV–I–V (A–D–A–E) turnaround. The best way to tackle complex phrasing like this is by approaching it one eighth note at a time, so work through each element of each phrase with specific attention to replicating the phrasing accurately.

Note that all of the notes sounded on the high E string are fingerpicked; he aggressively snaps the string against the fretboard by pulling up on it. And take special note of the beautiful vibrato that he executes on the high E string: slow and wide and played with a lot of emotion.

Honey Bee
From *Couldn't Stand the Weather*, 1984

This song is a hard-driving shuffle along the lines of tracks like "Pride and Joy," "I'm Crying," and "Look at Little Sister." Also played in the key of E (like all of the aforementioned songs), "Honey Bee" begins with a very cool *turnaround* phrase that is played over the V, IV, and I chords (B7, A7, and E7). For the B7 and A7 chords, Stevie plays lines based on B minor pentatonic and A minor pentatonic, respectively, with the 9th and ♭9th of each chord included, as well as their major 3rd (D♯ over B, and C♯ over A). The accompanying diagrams illustrate these scales, as well as the open-position E blues scale, which SRV relies on for his single-note lines over E7. In order to make tighter reference to the E dominant seventh tonality, he adds the major 3rd, G♯, to the E blues scale.

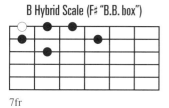

B Hybrid Scale (F♯ "B.B. box")

7fr

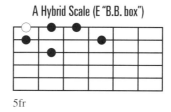

A Hybrid Scale (E "B.B. box")

5fr

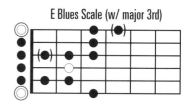

E Blues Scale (w/ major 3rd)

He begins over the B7 chord by sliding up to the major 3rd of B, D♯, and then plays the signature line based on the illustrated scales. The phrases over B7 and A7 can be analyzed as being in the style of both Freddie King and Lightnin' Hopkins. Also of note is that, when adding the 9th and ♭9th (C♯ and C) to B minor pentatonic, the resultant series of notes can also be thought of as the F♯ "B.B. Box" (D♯–F♯–A–B–C–C♯). Similarly, adding these intervals to A minor pentatonic results in the E "B.B. Box" (C♯–E–G–A–B♭–B), which is very useful, considering the song is played in the key of E.

Before attempting to play theses lines, listen closely to the recording and take note of Stevie's impeccable technique. When playing these lines, strive for the same crystal-clear articulation that he achieves.

Rude Mood
From *Texas Flood*, 1983

This uptempo shuffle, written by SRV, is heavily influenced by the song "Hopkins' Sky Hop." The song's signature theme, illustrated here, is based on a melodic line in the key of E major that is then transposed to A major when played over A, the IV chord. Instead of following the standard I–IV–V blues structure, an ascending phrase starting on the 2nd, F♯, is played in place of B, the V chord in the key of E.

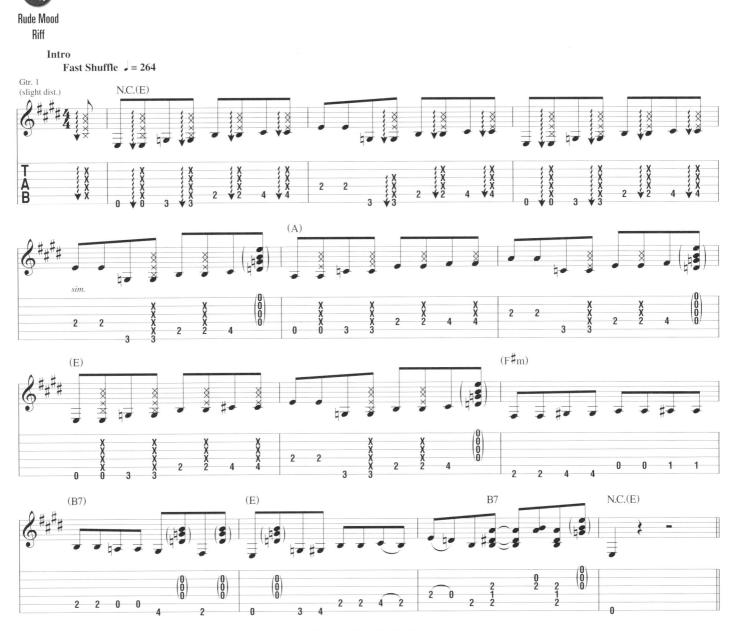

The accompanying diagrams illustrate the hybrid scales used over E and A. Over E, a riff based on E major pentatonic (E–F♯–G♯–B–C♯) is used; however, G, the minor 3rd, replaces G♯, the major 3rd. Likewise, over A, a riff based on A major pentatonic (A–B–C♯–E–F♯) is used but the minor 3rd, C, replaces the major 3rd, C♯.

E Major Pentatonic Scale (w/ ♭3rd)

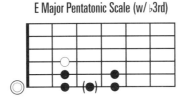

A Major Pentatonic Scale (w/ ♭3rd)

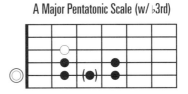

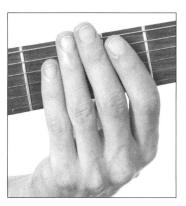

Be sure to use aggressive alternate picking throughout this phrase. You will notice that muted strings are sounded on virtually every other eighth note; Stevie accomplishes this by laying the fret-hand fingers across all of the strings while playing, sounding only the single note on each given string while dragging the pick across multiple strings (see photo).

Scuttle Buttin'
From *Couldn't Stand the Weather*, 1984

Like *Texas Flood*, a single 24-track two-inch machine was used to record SRV's sophomore effort, *Couldn't Stand the Weather*. The album kicks off with "Scuttle Buttin'," an absolute barn-burner—and a workout of blazing guitar virtuosity. "My brother Jimmie and I know that 'Scuttle Buttin'' is really just another way to play Lonnie Mack's 'Chicken Feed,'" Stevie told me back in 1986. Barely two minutes long, the song remained Stevie's set opener for many years and has since become *de riguer* for all aspiring blues and rock guitarists to try to master.

This song is based on a fast, repetitive riff that is played over each of the three chords of the I–IV–V progression in the key of E: E, A, and B. This phrase is based in the open-position E blues scale, as shown in the accompanying diagram.

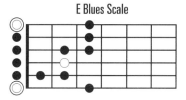

E Blues Scale

Starting with a downstroke, use alternate picking to execute this fast phrase. While Stevie used the middle finger of his fretting hand to fret all of the notes in the riff, feel free to use a different finger, or combination of fingers, if it feels more comfortable to you. After the riff is played each time, Stevie drops in the chord that is appropriate for that section of the I–IV–V progression, using E7#9 (no 3rd), A7, and B7. This is a very tricky riff, so I encourage you to begin by playing through the riff slowly, gradually increasing the tempo.

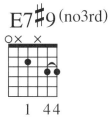

E7#9 (no3rd)

1 44

A7

1 1 1 4

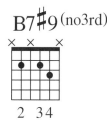

B7#9 (no3rd)

2 34

Scuttle Buttin'
Riff

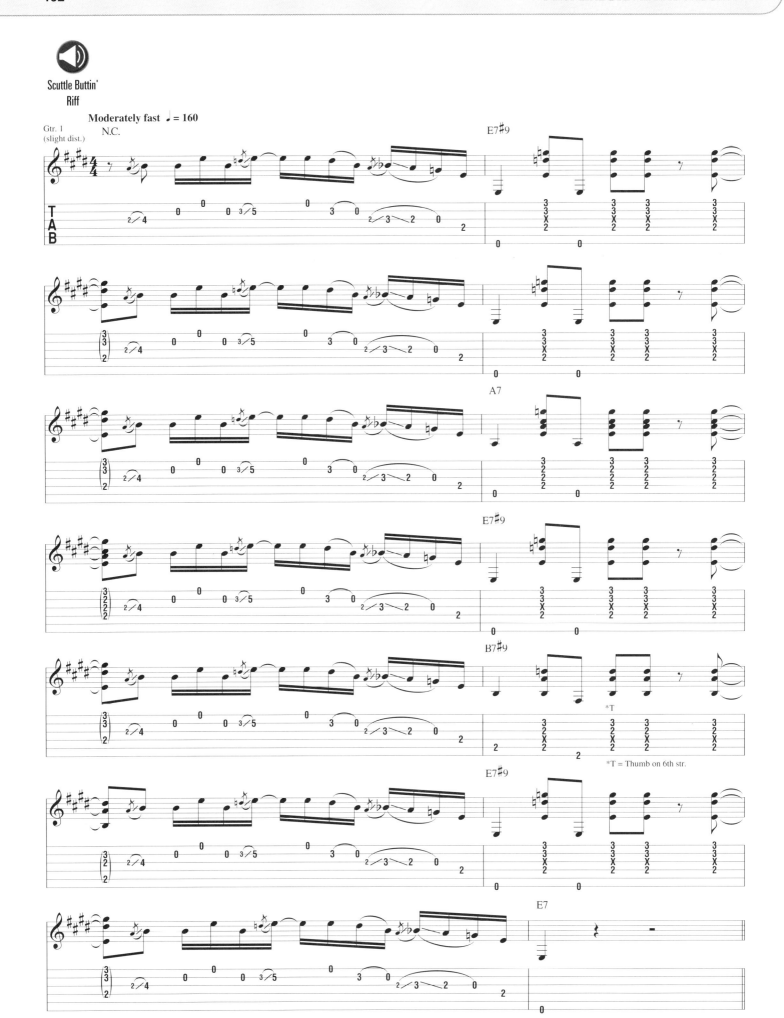

Wall of Denial
From *In Step*, 1989

This powerful track deals candidly with the rigors of drug rehabilitation and is built on insistently funky rhythm guitar lines borrowed from James Brown, with a twisting opening single-note riff that emulates Albert King's "Can't You See What You're Doing to Me," as well as Jimi Hendrix's "Jam Back at the House" (a.k.a. "Beginnings").

Included on his smash "comeback" album, *In Step* (1989), "Wall of Denial" addresses Stevie's struggles with substance abuse and the manner by which he successfully defeated his addictions. As difficult as this subject matter may have been, Stevie was determined to speak directly about this issue and it was imperative for him to get his point across. The song was co-written by Doyle Bramhall, Sr., who also co-wrote SRV classics like "Change It" and "Looking Out the Window."

The scale that this riff is based on can be most clearly analyzed as the E blues scale (E–G–A–Bb–B–D), wherein many of the G notes are bent up one half step in order to sound G#, the major 3rd of E. Use alternate picking throughout this riff and stick with the index and ring fingers for fretting in order to execute the phrase just as Stevie did. At the end of the phrase, he switches to an E9 chord (which slides up to F#9) and uses a down-up-down strumming pattern that is based on eighth-note triplets.

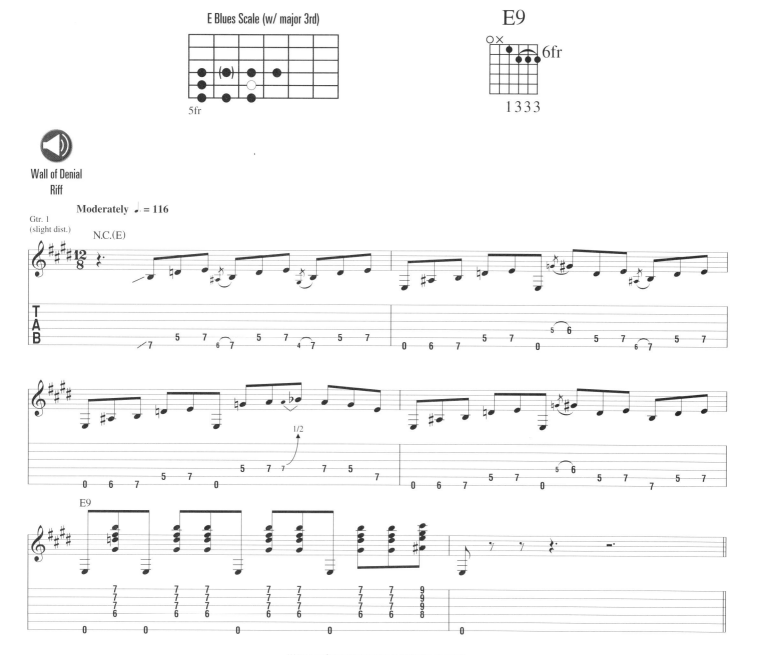

Empty Arms
From *Soul to Soul*, 1985

"Empty Arms" is an SRV original that Stevie recorded in two drastically different arrangements, only one of which was released during his lifetime. The originally issued "Empty Arms" features Stevie Ray on both drums and guitar and is performed at a very slow tempo. Recorded during the *Soul to Soul* sessions, the track was played so slowly that it was ultimately sped-up by a VSO (variable speed oscillator) to the tempo heard on the recording. But he also recorded a live in the studio version in 1984, played at a faster tempo and with an uptempo swing treatment, and it is that version that is represented here. His playing on this take is razor sharp in its precision and beautifully musical in its delivery and is certainly an essential track for any true SRV fan.

The majority of Stevie's soloing is based on the C blues scale (C–Eb–F–Gb–G–Bb), with the inclusion of the major 3rd, E, the 6th, A, and the 9th, D, reflecting the C Mixolydian mode very closely. The accompanying diagrams illustrate both the C blues scale with the added major 3rd and the C Mixolydian mode.

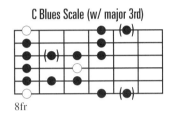

C Blues Scale (w/ major 3rd)

8fr

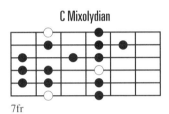

C Mixolydian

7fr

The example below represents the "Empty Arms" intro, which kicks off with a solo guitar single-note pickup lick. One of the tricky things about this pickup is that the first note comes in on the upbeat of beat 3. Played in a moderately fast tempo and 4/4 time with a "triplet feel" equivalency (lines written as straight eighth notes are played as a quarter note/eighth note couplet within an eighth-note triplet bracket), the minor 3rd, Eb, is sounded on the upbeat of beat 3 and hammered onto the major 3rd, E, on the downbeat of beat 4. In the subsequent (first) bar, the b7th, Bb, is sounded squarely on the downbeat of beat 1. I make mention of this because the lick is often misinterpreted as the first note, Eb, sounding on the upbeat of beat *four*, with the major 3rd, E, sounding on the downbeat of beat 1 of the first bar. The chordal accents then fall on the upbeats of beat 2 in the following bars.

Once again, Stevie executes this lick with absolute clarity and precision, so strive to replicate his smooth and effortless articulation. Once the bass and drums enter in bar 5 of this excerpt, SRV switches to sliding double-stop sixths and triple-stop ninths based on the three chords of the I–IV–V progression in the key of C: C6–F9–G9.

Lenny
From *Texas Flood*, 1983

"Lenny" is a beautiful, Hendrix-inspired ballad that Stevie wrote for his first wife, Lenora. The solo section is made up of alternating bars of Emaj13 and Amaj9; stylistically, the song is similar to Jimi Hendrix's classic ballad "Angel."

The beautiful chords that Stevie utilizes throughout this track are 13th and sixth chords, starting with the repetitive E13–A6 progression that comprises the "verse" section of the tune. For E13, the fret-hand pinky is used to barre across the top two strings at the ninth fret to sound the major 3rd, G#, and the 13th (sixth), C#. It may take some practice to become accustomed to switching comfortably between these two voicings, so practice fretting each chord carefully, as well as learning to switch between the two chords seamlessly.

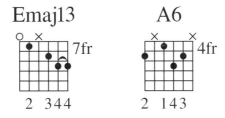

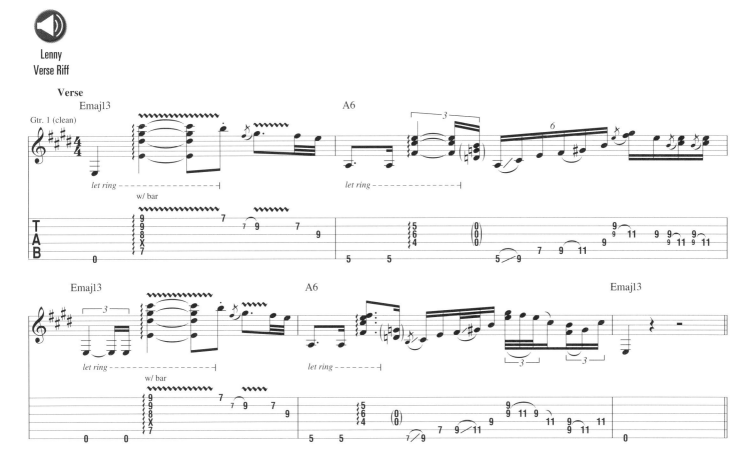

Lenny
Verse Riff

Written by Stevie Ray Vaughan

Here's the "bridge" section to "Lenny," along with chord diagrams that illustrate all of the chords used throughout the section.

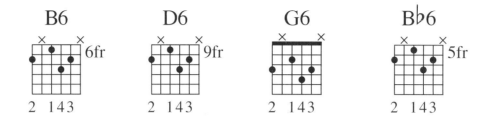

Lenny
Bridge Riff

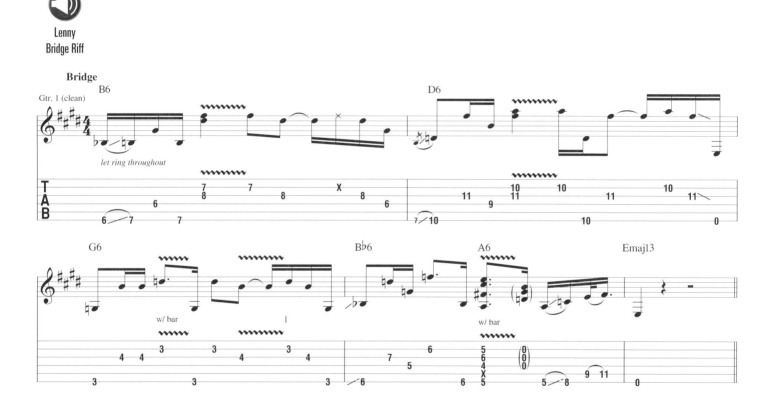

Of great importance is the subtle use of hammer-ons, pull-offs, and slides throughout, which serve to provide a "liquid" feel to his well-articulated and melodic phrases. When playing these lines, Stevie sticks with the index and ring fingers of his fret hand.

Look at Little Sister
From *Soul to Soul*, 1985

Here's another hard-driving "thunder shuffle" along the lines of Stevie's signature tune, "Pride and Joy." Also played in the key of E, the lion's share of the verse's guitar part (shown here) is built from root–5th and root–6th (and the occasional root–♭7th) voicings on either the E and A strings or the A and D strings. Stevie picks this figure very aggressively, using downstrokes exclusively.

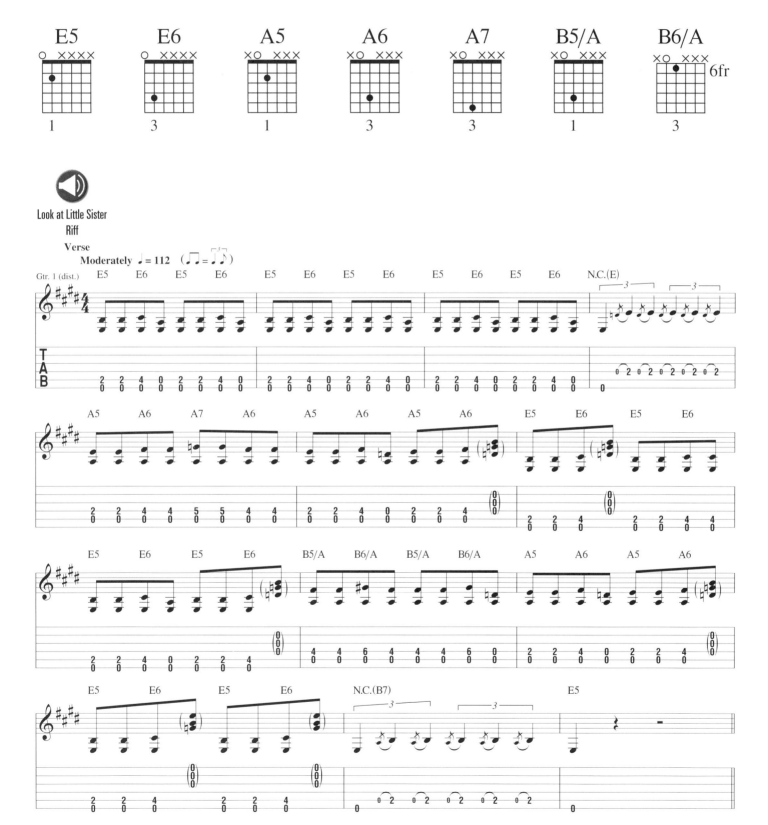

At the end of each 12-bar verse form, Stevie plays improvised figures based on the E blues scale (the accompanying diagram illustrates this scale in open position). When listening to the SRV recording, notice the smooth execution of slides, hammer-ons, and pull-offs, all employed to accentuate the bluesy, greasy feel of the tune.

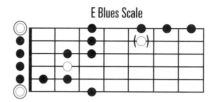

E Blues Scale

Riviera Paradise
From *In Step*, 1989

"Riviera Paradise" reveals Stevie's love of jazz guitar and the influence of jazz greats Wes Montgomery, Kenny Burrell, Grant Green, Jackie King, and Fred Walters. Stevie had written the song well before cutting the incredible version included on his last studio recording, *In Step*, combining complex chordal work with beautifully simple and melodic soloing.

All of the chord forms used during the verse section (there are eight different voicings used) are shown in the accompanying diagrams. Of interest is that the initial chord shape used for Em9 places the minor 3rd, G, as the lowest fretted note (or, "in the bass"). Subsequently, this chord shape is re-imagined with the lowest note representing the root note: in bar 5, the initial chord "grip" shifts down two frets but, instead of representing Dm9, an F is played by bassist Tommy Shannon, implying Fmaj7. In this way, the structure of the chord progression in bars 1–4 shifts from i–IV (Em9–A13) to ♭VII–I (Fmaj7–Gmaj7). The progression ends with a iim7♭5–V7♯9/♭9 (F♯m7♭5–B7♯9/♭9), which is commonly known as a ii–V resolution back to the I chord, Em9.

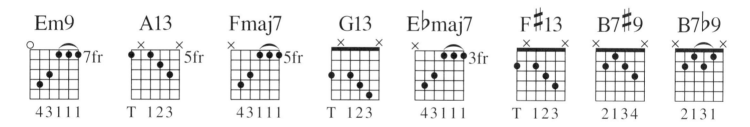

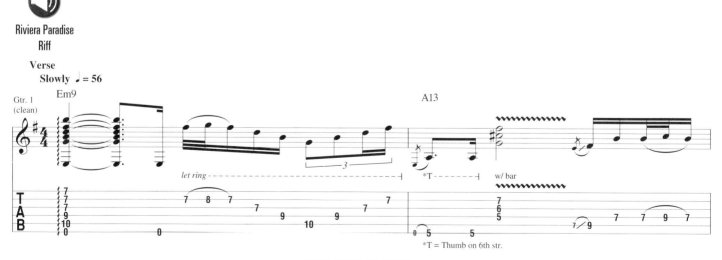

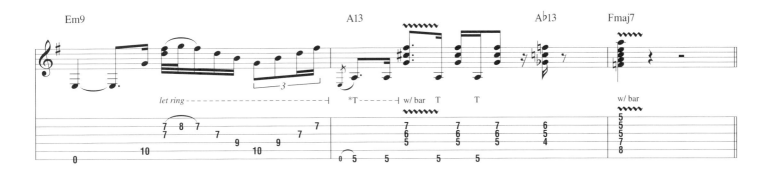

The Sky Is Crying
From *The Sky Is Crying*, 1991

Elmore James's slow-blues hit "The Sky Is Crying" (1959) is one of the most widely covered blues songs of all time. Albert King recorded a seminal version of the song for his *Years Gone By* album (1969), and no doubt Stevie studied this recording intensely during his formative years as a blues guitarist. Stevie performs the song in the key of C and relies on the C blues scale for the majority of the licks and phrases that he plays during the verse and solo sections of the song. The accompanying diagrams illustrate the C blues scale as played in the eighth-fret box pattern, as well as in an extended pattern.

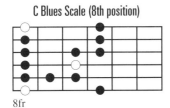

C Blues Scale (8th position)

8fr

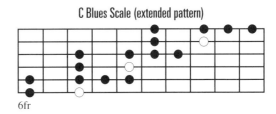

C Blues Scale (extended pattern)

6fr

The following excerpt represents the first verse of "The Sky Is Crying." Throughout the verses, Stevie utilizes "call and response" technique whereby he "answers" all of his vocal phrases with short, improvised single-note blues lines that are very much indicative of the strong influence of Albert King's soloing style. In bar 1, he initiates his first lick by quickly bending the 4th, F, up one whole step to G on the high E string, fingerpicking for added emphasis. This is followed by the note F (13th fret) and quick movement from E♭ to C and from B♭ to G. Next, a quick whole-step bend moves from F to G on the G string and is followed by a stinging high-C root note, also fingerpicked (and heavily vibratoed). Stevie returns to the high F-to-G bend throughout this first verse but, in bars 7–8, he shifts to eighth position and plays faster, more complex lines that reflect his distinct approach to the blues, which includes perfect execution, speed, and precision, as well as deep feeling. Also note the very subtle use of the Roland Dimension D flanging effect that Stevie had employed on such tracks as "Pride and Joy" and "Mary Had a Little Lamb," as well as many other tracks.

The Sky Is Crying
Riff

Verse
Slow Blues ♩ = 55

INTEGRAL TECHNIQUES

SRV possessed the kind of guitar technique that most players can only dream of. In this section, we will break down the intricacies of his brilliant pick- and fret-hand techniques.

All fans of SRV are well familiar with his penchant for using very heavy string gauges. Suffice it to say, bending heavier strings, like .012s or .013s, is more difficult and requires more strength than bending "standard" electric string gauges like .009s or .010s. To reiterate, Stevie mentioned in many interviews that he preferred these gauges: .013, .015, .019, .028, .038, .058 (high to low), tuned down one half step (low to high: E♭–A♭–D♭–G♭–B♭–E♭). Rene Martinez, Stevie's tech of many years, told me that for the last few tours, Stevie often switched to a .012 or an .011 for the high E string to reduce the chances of tearing off the ends of his fingertips, as he often did (Stevie's MASH unit-style Krazy Glue repair of his fingertips is one of legend).

Stevie explained his preference for such heavy gauges thusly: "They don't *move*! They stay in tune better than lighter-gauge strings and they won't bend unintentionally while I'm playing." Stevie utilized the advantages of heavy-gauge strings by oftentimes relying on slides and pull-offs in many of his riffs in lieu of bending, resulting in beautifully liquid phrasing and expertly executed fast legato licks and patterns.

The Slide/Pull-Off

Example 1 illustrates a basic slide/pull-off: using the ring finger to fret the first note, slide the finger up one fret and then back to the original fret, pulling off to the index finger positioned two frets lower on the same string. Additionally, add a slight quarter-step bend on the last note, C, to lend a blues-ier, more vocal sound to the riff. As shown, repeat this movement many times in order to master it. Start slowly and be sure to sound every note as clearly as possible.

Techniques
Example 1

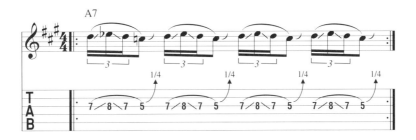

Now let's expand on this basic idea by adding more notes to the end of the phrase. In Example 2, the slide/pull-off is executed as 32nd notes and a low-A root note is added at the end of the hand movement.

Techniques
Example 2

In Example 3, two notes are added to the initial phrase, resulting in a quintuplet (five-note) figure, followed by a return to a quarter-step bent C note.

Techniques
Example 3

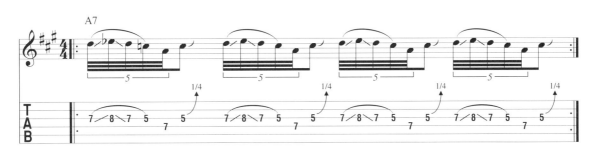

In Example 4, the repeated phrase from Example 2 is alternated against a fast pull-off lick that moves across the D and A strings.

Techniques Example 4

Play these figures over and over until they sound as silky smooth as SRV. Great examples can be found on slow-tempo tracks like "Tin Pan Alley" and "Little Wing."

We can combine the sliding movement on the G string with additional notes on the B string to result in Example 5, which is a "cycling" figure that Stevie used very often. Once you have it down, try playing this figure with a 12/8 time signature, against a very slow tempo, as one would do when playing a slow blues.

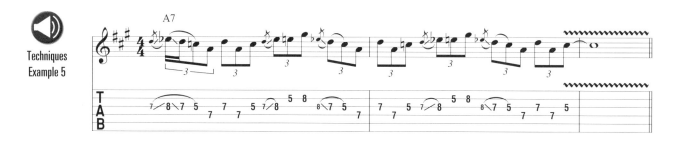

Techniques Example 5

Example 6 offers an even more complex application of the slide/pull-off technique, expanded to a "cramming"-type riff very much in the style of Jimi Hendrix that Stevie would often use for everything from a slow blues to "Mary Had a Little Lamb" to "Cold Shot."

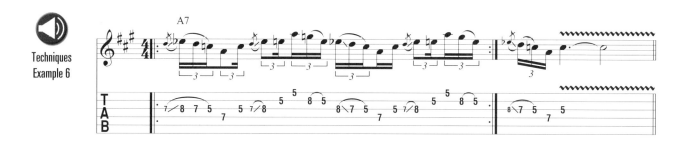

Techniques Example 6

Oblique Hammer/Slide/Pull-Off (à la Buddy Guy)

Another way to incorporate the slide/pull-off is to add a high root-note pedal tone on top, as SRV's hero Buddy Guy often did, heard on such classic tracks as "First Time I Met the Blues."

As shown in Example 7 and played in the key of B minor, a slide/pull-off is executed on the G string while a high root note is sounded simultaneously on the high E string. Barre the fret-hand index finger across the seventh fret of the top three strings, and while using the pick to strike the G string, fingerpick the high E string with the middle or ring finger of the pick hand. It can be tricky to get the G and high-E strings to sound clearly, so listen closely and focus on your articulation techniques.

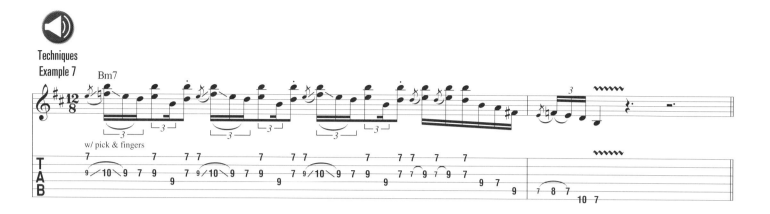

Techniques
Example 7

String Bending

Whole- and Half-Step Bends

Mastering blues guitar soloing requires an expert's touch, especially when it comes to string bending, and Stevie Ray was one of the best ever at a great variety of string-bending techniques. The goal when string-bending is to achieve perfect *intonation* (i.e., all bends sound perfectly in tune). The following examples, all played in SRV's style, will help you to perfect your string-bending capabilities.

Examples 8–11 are all played in the key of G over a slow-blues feel along the lines of "Texas Flood." Let's begin with a single whole-step bend, as shown in Example 8: bend the first note, C, up one whole step to D and then play the unbent C note on the next beat.

Techniques
Example 8

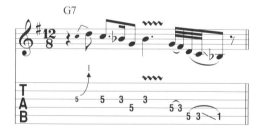

In Example 9, the riff begins with the same whole-step bend, but the C note is sounded by bending upward one *half* step from the B note below it. As such, the lick offers a good exercise for practicing whole- and half-step bends within the same phrase.

Techniques
Example 9

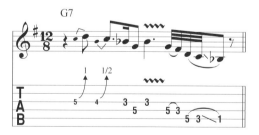

In Example 10, this idea is expanded upon in a slightly more complex phrase that once again combines whole- and half-step bends.

Techniques
Example 10

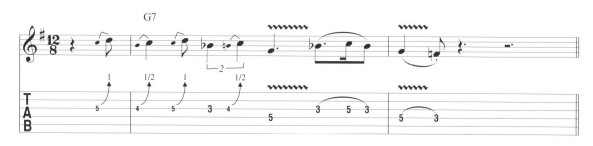

In Example 11, the initial bends from the previous licks are moved up one octave, to the high E string, followed in bar 2 by whole-step bends on the G string.

Techniques Example 11

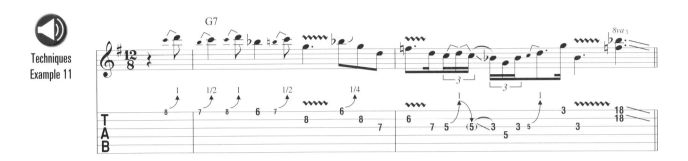

Overbends

Albert King, one of Stevie's idols, was the master of the *overbend*, oftentimes bending notes one-and-a-half or two steps. Albert would tune his guitar down one-and-a-half steps, resulting in slinky strings that were relatively easy to bend, so Stevie had to come up with different ways to emulate that sound via standard string-bending. But Stevie also would use one-and-a-half and two-step bends regularly.

Example 12 illustrates a riff along the lines of what Stevie would play during his solo on "Voodoo Chile (Slight Return)." Following the whole-step bend on the G string and the move across the B and high-E strings, a high G note is alternately bent one-and-a-half steps and one whole step before settling on a vibratoed minor 3rd, G, and a move back down to the G string. Be sure to listen closely while executing these bends, striving for sharp clarity between the two types of bends.

Techniques Example 12

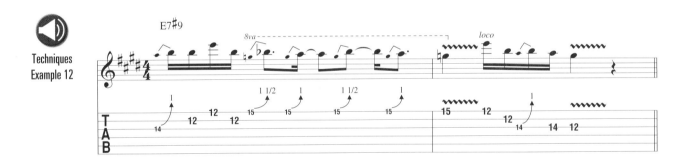

Example 13 is also played over a "Voodoo Chile"-type groove, but here, the initial bend on the high E string is a two-step overbend, executed gradually to accentuate the "travel" of the note. Once again, listen closely and strive for perfect intonation.

Techniques Example 13

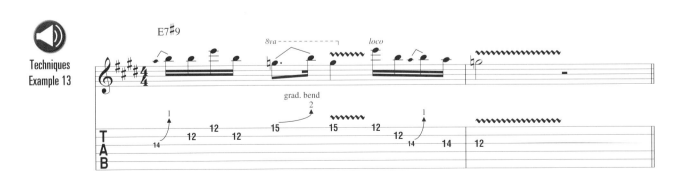

Vibrato

Stevie Ray Vaughan possessed a very distinct vibrato—powerful, slow, and wide, evoking a deep blues feeling and musicality. Combined with the greatest Stratocaster tone imaginable, his vibratos always sounded majestic, whether executing single notes, bent vibratos, or oblique bend/vibratos.

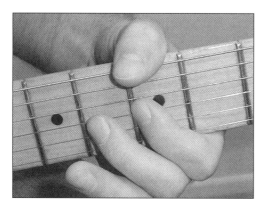

Example 14 represents a slow blues in the key of A, and here, all of the vibratos are executed with the fret-hand index finger. Starting with the first C note, the vibrato is sounded by keeping the index finger stiff while positioning the side of the index finger (by the knuckle) against the underside of the neck and then rocking the finger back and forth evenly, using the bottom of the neck as a *fulcrum* (see photo). It will take diligent practice to sound a smooth, wide, and even vibrato as Stevie does. The C is then repeated on beat 3 and moved down an octave (to the A string) on beat 1 of the next bar. You will notice that adding a vibrato on a wound string requires a little more energy than when adding vibrato to an unwound string.

Techniques
Example 14

Example 15 is also played with a slow-blues feel (think "Ain't Gone 'N' Give Up on Love"), but here, the initial vibrato is moved over to the high E string. Be sure to rock the string in an *upward* motion, towards the center of the fretboard, while applying vibrato. This riff ends with vibrato on the C note on the low E string, fretted with the pinky. This brings up a good point: as a matter of daily practice, play vibratoed notes with all four of the fret-hand fingers, striving for identical execution of each vibrato.

Techniques
Example 15

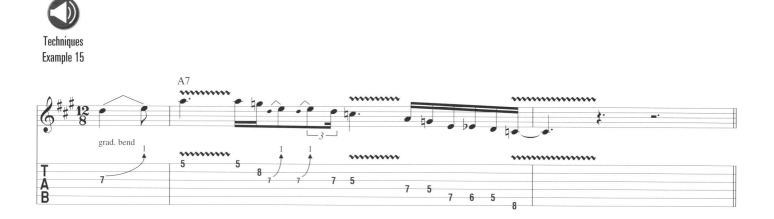

This next example gives you a chance to practice your ring-finger vibrato. Example 16 represents a lick along the lines of one Stevie plays on the uptempo version of "Empty Arms." After the initial ring-finger bend on the G string and the move across the higher strings, the ring finger is used to apply vibrato to the high E♭ at the beginning of bar 2. The ring finger is also used for the vibratoed C note at the end of the bar and the C note one octave lower at the end of bar 3.

Techniques
Example 16

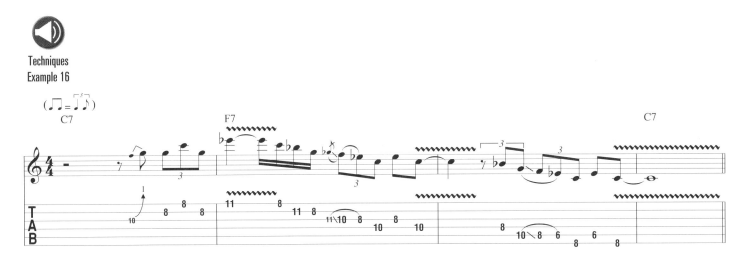

Bent Vibratos

This is another essential technique in the SRV arsenal. As expressive as bends and vibratos are, bent vibratos have a feeling and a "vibe" all of their own. This is a difficult technique to master and will take hours of diligent practice to learn to do with precision and control.

"Cold Shot" is another song with a deep, dark, heavy blues feel that is perfectly suited to bent vibratos. Example 17 is played in this style, starting with whole-step bent vibratos on the high-E string. Use the ring finger for these bends, keeping the middle and index fingers lined up along the E string, behind the fretting finger, which helps to reinforce the bend as well as solidify the vibrato.

Techniques
Example 17

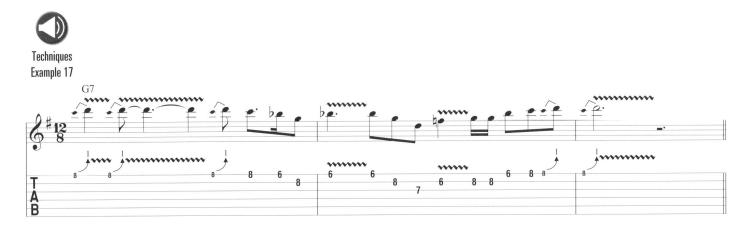

Example 18 is in the key of A minor and opens with bent vibrato on the G string and closes with index-finger vibrato, also on the G string.

Techniques
Example 18

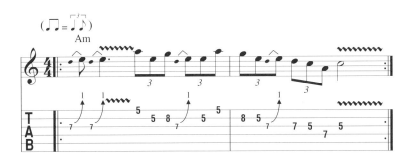

Tremolo Picking

This is another technique that Stevie took to an entirely new dimension. Tremolo picking involves picking a single note or group of notes in a very rapid and repetitive manner, most often faster than something that could be written in, say 32nd or 64th notes. The symbol located above or below the notehead and through the stem indicates that the note should be tremolo picked. On slow blues songs like "Dirty Pool" and "Tin Pan Alley," Stevie tremolo picks groups of notes with a circular pick-hand motion that he would refer to as a "figure eight." Most guitarists, however, simply strum with the pick in a fast alternating (down-up) motion.

Example 19 illustrates a lick in B minor along the lines of SRV's "Dirty Pool" solo, wherein triads (three-note chords) are sounded with slides and tremolo picking. Strum across the strings with the pick hand as quickly and evenly as possible, applying very little pressure with the pick. When executed properly, it should feel like you are simply "brushing" the strings. Once you have the technique down, try tremolo picking single notes and double stops as well.

Techniques
Example 19

Repetitive Licks

It is a staple of the blues guitar soloing language to take a three- or four-note lick and "cycle" it over and over, effectively creating a sense of tension until the figure is resolved with a "closing" statement. Stevie Ray's incredible technique came into play in this regard in a great many of his solos. One of the greatest examples that comes to mind is his brilliant playing on the live version of "Lenny" from the *Live at El Mocambo* DVD. Let's take a look at a few standard SRV-approved phrases that he would cycle in a repetitive manner.

SRV played many songs in the key of E—"Pride and Joy" and "Voodoo Chile" are great examples—and he would often blaze through repetitive patterns during his solos on these songs. In Example 20, only the index finger is used to fret all of the notes, starting at the second fret of the G string and then sliding up to the third fret, back to the second fret, and then pulling off to the open G string, followed by E on the second fret of the fourth string. This 32nd-note phrase is followed by a triplet phrase using the notes A, E, and G, after which the one-beat pattern is repeated.

Techniques
Example 20

In Example 21, the 32nd-note index-finger sliding figure is cycled alone. When played fast, this is a very flashy-sounding lick that can be used over everything from a slow blues to a fast shuffle.

Techniques
Example 21

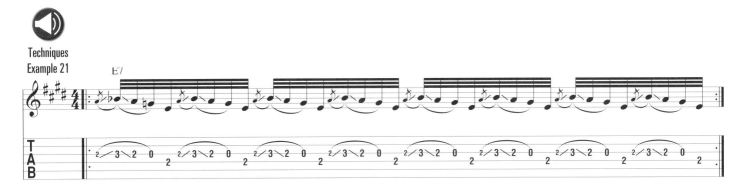

Speaking of shuffles, Stevie played a great many blues shuffles in the key of E—"Pride and Joy," "I'm Crying," "Look at Little Sister," etc.—and Example 22 offers a Lightnin' Hopkins-style riff based on repeatedly sliding up to B and D notes on the third and second strings, respectively, after which these two notes are joined by the open high-E string and played in a repetitive eighth-note triplet rhythm.

Techniques
Example 22

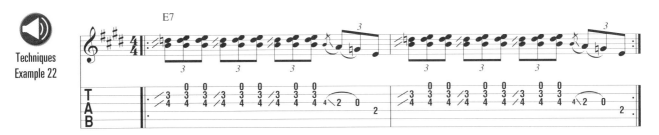

Now let's examine some closed-position (no open strings) repetitive phrases. Example 23 is a lick built from 16th-note triplets and based on the A minor pentatonic scale (A–C–D–E–G). With the index finger barred across the top two strings at the fifth fret, use the ring finger to bend the notes fretted on the seventh and eighth frets of the G and B strings, respectively. Notice also the pull-offs that occur repeatedly on the G string; Stevie would normally sound these with his ring and index fingers.

Techniques
Example 23

In Example 24, we build on the idea introduced in Example 23 by playing a lick built entirely from pairs of 16th-note triplets (sextuplets). This lick includes the quick hammer/pull between the ♭9th, B♭, and the root note, A, in the style of blues guitar great T-Bone Walker. "Say What?" is a great example of a tune on which Stevie would cycle a lick like this at blazing speed.

Techniques
Example 24

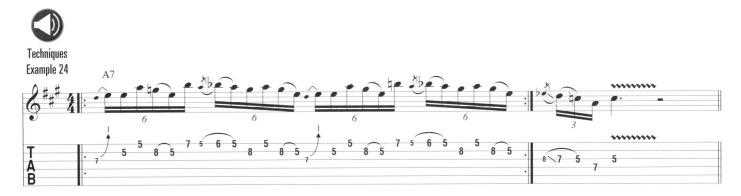

STYLISTIC DNA

All of the greatest instrumentalists have a sound that is their own—distinct and immediately recognizable. In this section, we will look at that aspect of SRV's approach and sound on the guitar.

Slow-Blues Phrasing

Stevie cut a great many slow-blues tracks in the studio, and every live show contained a handful of slow-blues songs on which he would display his stunning virtuosity as a blues soloist. Some of his greatest slow-blues performances are "Texas Flood," "Ain't Gone 'N' Give Up on Love," "Leave My Girl Alone," "Tin Pan Alley," "The Sky Is Crying," "Dirty Pool," and "May I Have a Talk With You," among others.

Examples 1–2 are both played in the key of G and represent licks that Stevie used on the studio version of "Texas Flood." The first thing to keep in mind is that slow blues is usually written in 12/8 meter, so three evenly spaced eighth notes fall on each of the four beats in each bar. Always keep this "framework" in mind when navigating through complex solo phrases like those shown here, as this will make reading and understanding the "internal" rhythms (16th notes, 16th-note triplets, etc.) easier.

Example 1 begins with straight 16th notes played in third position, so the index finger is barred across the top two strings at the third fret while the ring finger is used for bends on any note located at the fifth or sixth fret. Half-step bends at the fourth fret are fretted with the middle finger. Even within a short two-bar phrase like this, there resides a great variety of rhythmic subdivision of the eighth-note triplets, so read through the phrase slowly and listen to the recording repeatedly while attempting to master the phrase.

DNA
Example 1

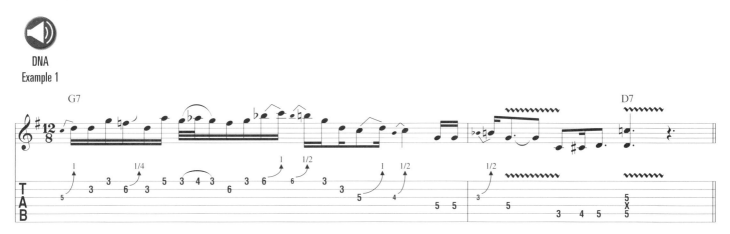

Example 2 begins in a similar manner, except the ascent to the high G happens much quicker, followed by a shift to sixth position via a ring-finger slide. This shift places the fretting fingers in perfect position for the licks that fall on beat 3, after which the index finger is used for the multiple bends and subsequent slide back down to third position. This phrase ends with a classic "fall off" lick, as G is pulled off to F, followed by a low D. You will hear "fall off" licks like this one in just about every slow blues recorded by Jimi Hendrix ("Red House" is a perfect example).

DNA
Example 2

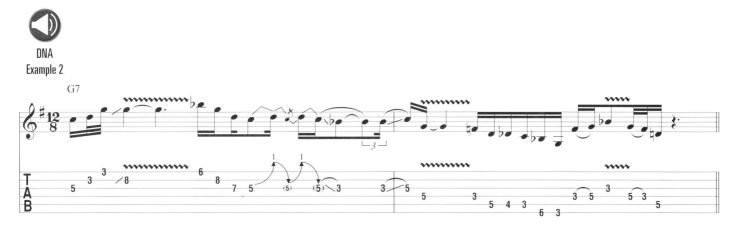

"Snapping" the Strings

One of the most distinct signatures of the great Albert King was the way in which he'd "snap" the strings against the fretboard when soloing. Albert always picked with his fingers (and played the guitar "lefty," with the strings upside down), so he would use his gigantic thumb to aggressively pick notes on the high E string, briefly lifting the string up as he picked it and then letting it go, effectively snapping it against the fretboard for a sharp and intense sound. SRV emulated this sound better than anyone (Albert didn't mind; he routinely referred to Stevie as his "god son") and used the technique on just about every song that he recorded.

Example 3 represents a two-bar phrase played in the context of a slow blues in G, à la "Texas Flood" or "The Things (That) I Used to Do." All notes that are fretted on the high E string are sounded by fingerpicking with the pick-hand middle finger: the string is lifted up with each attack and snapped down against the fretboard. Play through this phrase slowly and strive for a smooth transition between "snapped" notes and notes that are picked conventionally.

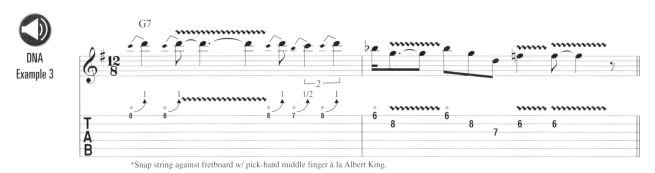

DNA
Example 3

*Snap string against fretboard w/ pick-hand middle finger à la Albert King.

Example 4 is along the lines of Stevie's soloing on the slow blues "Ain't Gone 'N' Give Up on Love," played in the key of A. In this lick, the notes move more frequently between the high E string and the B and G strings, so once again, strive for an even and precise transition between fingerpicked notes and notes that are flat-picked.

DNA
Example 4

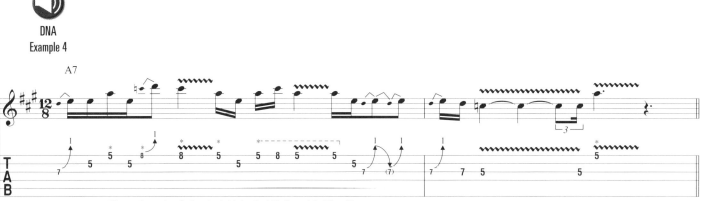

*Snap string against fretboard w/ pick-hand middle finger à la Albert King.

Oblique Bends

An *oblique bend* is a figure wherein one bent note is played simultaneously with one or more unbent notes. This essential tool in every blues player's bag is something Stevie Ray utilized to great effect on some of his greatest solos.

Example 5 is a lick played in the style of Stevie's soloing on "Cold Shot," a slow, swinging blues that, in this example, is written in straight eighth notes with a "triplet equivalency," which means that notes written as straight eighths are intended to be played as a quarter note/eighth note pair within an eighth-note triplet bracket. The specific oblique bend featured here involves a note on the G string, which is bent one whole step and sounded simultaneously with a fretted note on the high E string. Hybrid picking is necessary in order to strike the third and first strings simultaneously: use the pick on the third string and fingerpick the high E string. The distinct sound of the oblique bend is a signature of this solo, as SRV leans on the technique repeatedly.

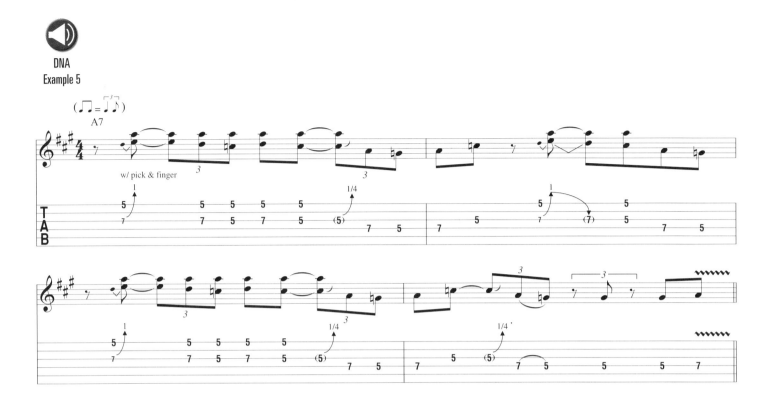

DNA
Example 5

Another great example of SRV employing oblique bends can be found on his solo from "Couldn't Stand the Weather." Example 6 is played in this style, as notes bent on the G string are allowed to ring into notes fretted conventionally on the B and high-E strings.

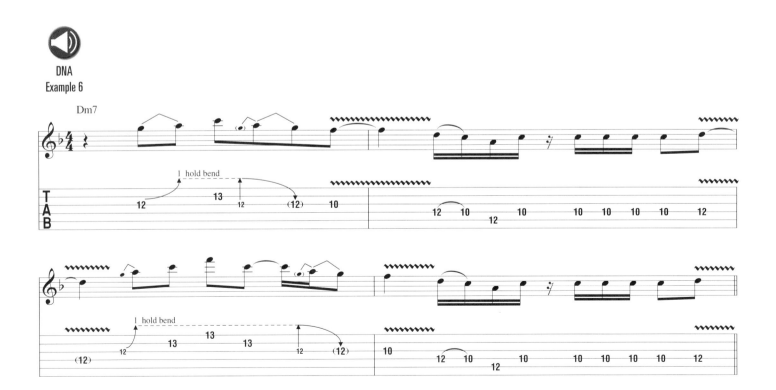

DNA
Example 6

Double Stops and Trills

Let's wrap up this section with a look at two more essential SRV-approved techniques: double stops and trills. A *double stop* is the term used to describe when two notes are sounded simultaneously. A *trill* involves the rapid back-and-forth movement between two notes, usually fretted on the same string.

Example 7 represents a lick that Stevie used on the song "Love Struck Baby," wherein he plays descending double stops in the style of Chuck Berry (à la "Johnny B. Goode"). When playing licks like these, Stevie would fret exclusively with the ring and index fingers, dragging the ring finger down the pair of notes on the high-E and B strings and the B and G strings.

DNA
Example 7

Example 8 is played in the style of the primary lick in "Couldn't Stand the Weather." With the fret-hand thumb wrapped around the top of the fretboard to fret the low-D root note (sixth string, 10th fret), the index, ring, and pinky are all used to barre across pairs of strings in order to sound two or three notes simultaneously. Proper pick-hand technique is required here, as the pick must alternate quickly between low and high strings in order to articulate the phrase cleanly.

DNA
Example 8

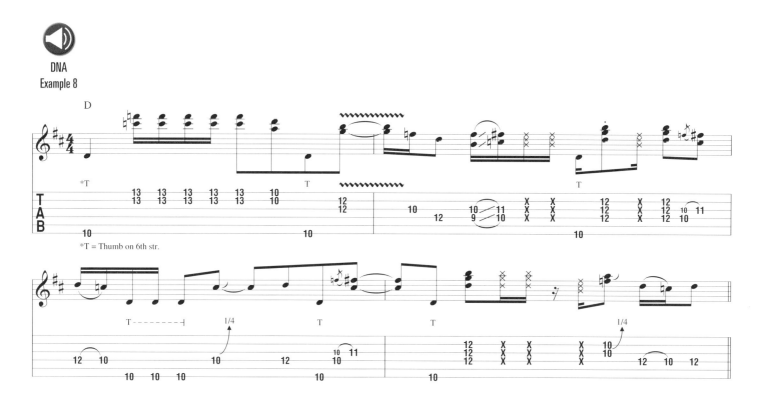

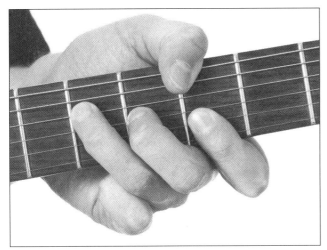

Example 9 represents the intro to the song "Say What?," during which Stevie quickly trills between Bb and C on the D string while simultaneously fretting a low C by wrapping the fret-hand thumb around the top of the fretboard. A firm grip is required, so hold the neck baseball bat-style while keeping the index and ring fingers relaxed enough to trill (hammer on and pull off) quickly between the eighth and 10th frets (see photo). The phrase ends with an additional trill between Eb and E while a Bb is fretted simultaneously below the trill.

DNA
Example 9

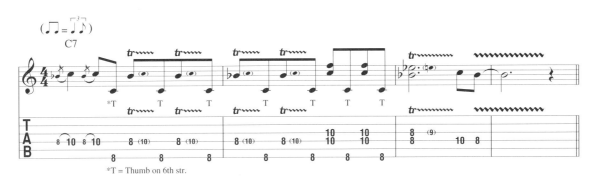

*T = Thumb on 6th str.

MUST HEAR

For any true fan of Stevie Ray Vaughan—and any true aspiring blues or blues-rock guitarist—an "essential listening" list would be *every single thing* that Stevie ever played on. Below is a select discography, albeit one that is very broad and represents his most well-known recordings, as well as some great collections.

Audio Recordings

Let's Dance (David Bowie), 1983

Essential Tracks

Let's Dance
China Girl
Cat People

Texas Flood, 1983

Essential Tracks

Texas Flood
Love Struck Baby
Pride and Joy
Lenny
Rude Mood

Couldn't Stand the Weather, 1984

Essential Tracks

Scuttle Buttin'
Couldn't Stand the Weather
Voodoo Chile (Slight Return)
Cold Shot

Soul To Soul, 1985

Essential Tracks

Say What?
Change It
Life Without You
Ain't Gone 'N' Give Up on Love
Look at Little Sister

Live Alive, 1986

Essential Tracks

I'm Leaving You (Commit a Crime)
Willie the Wimp
Texas Flood

In Step, 1989
Essential Tracks

Crossfire
Tightrope
Wall of Denial
Riviera Paradise

Family Style, 1990
Essential Tracks

D/FW
Tick Tock
Telephone Song

The Sky Is Crying, 1991
Essential Tracks

The Sky Is Crying
Empty Arms
Little Wing
May I Have a Talk With You
Life by the Drop
Chitlins Con Carne

In the Beginning, 1992
Essential Tracks

In the Open
Tin Pan Alley
Shake for Me

Live at Carnegie Hall, 1997
Essential Tracks

Cold Shot
Dirty Pool
Iced Over (Collins' Shuffle)
Lenny

In Session (with Albert King), 1999
Essential Tracks

Call It Stormy Monday
Ask Me No Questions
Blues at Sunrise

SRV (box set), 2000
Essential Tracks

Thunderbird
Don't Lose Your Cool
Manic Depression
Hug You, Squeeze You
Little Wing/Third Stone from the Sun
Boilermaker
Leave My Girl Alone

Live at Montreux: 1982 & 1985, 2001
Essential Tracks

Hide Away
Rude Mood
Texas Flood
Ain't Gone 'N' Give Up on Love
Tin Pan Alley
Voodoo Chile (Slight Return)
Life Without You

Texas Hurricane (vinyl box set), 2012
Essential Tracks

Pride and Joy
Couldn't Stand the Weather
Say What?
Crossfire
Empty Arms

MUST SEE

There is no better way to gain insight into the true power and greatness of Stevie Ray Vaughan's incredible virtuosity than by watching videos of his live performances. Below is a collection of the most highly recommended.

On DVD

Pride and Joy, 1991

Live at El Mocambo, 1991

Live from Austin, Texas, 1995

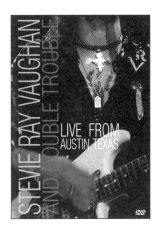

Live at Montreux: 1982 & 1985, 2004

In Session (with Albert King), 2010

On YouTube

Live at the Capital Theater, 1985

Live at Rockpalast, 1985

Live in Tokyo, 1985

Live at Daytona Beach, 1987

Live in Nashville, 1987

Live in New Orleans, Jazz and Heritage Festival, 1987

Live in Pistoia Italy, 1988

Live on MTV Unplugged, 1990